Praise for
The Q-Loop and Brian Klapper

"*The Q-Loop* is the rare 'how to' book that provides a step-by-step action plan for achieving transformational change. In my 30 years working with Six Sigma, ISO, and Kaizen, I've never seen anything as effective at driving operational efficiency as the work pioneered by Brian Klapper. In addition, because of his work with us, our customer service scores and employee satisfaction are rising. We are far from finished but what I will have in the end is a culture of process improvement and an organization that is much more scalable and operationally efficient."

—David Castellani, CEO, New York Life Retirement Plan Services

"This book takes the change bull by the horns—it gets directly at what management needs to *do* to tee up and implement productive change, rather than announce yet another change program."

—Ian MacMillan, PhD, the Dhirubhai Ambani Professor of Innovation and Entrepreneurship; Director, Sol C. Snider Entrepreneurial Research Center, Wharton Graduate School of Business

"Brian Klapper weaves together two seemingly unrelated disciplines, the hard science of operational transformation with the art of behavioral change, to create a breakthrough approach to corporate transformation. *The Q-Loop* is an innovator's guide to accelerating transformational change and more importantly, making it stick. If you are involved with any aspect of business transformation, you will read it, reference it, and use it as a daily companion."

—Tom Kelly, CEO, Silpada Designs

"*The Q-Loop* combines two critical elements for achieving real results— a practical methodology rather than a bunch of theory, and a unique approach to accelerate implementation. Change is hard and the Q-Loop model helped us meet our aggressive goals."

—Dave Benson, CIO, Progress Software

"We've employed the Q-Loop for roughly three years now and can honestly say that it has positively contributed to our culture of change by enabling ownership and accountability to be better distributed throughout our organization. The approach has also generated a consistent series of relatively quick 'wins,' which has directly translated into dramatic bottom-line results. This has reinforced our vision and motivated participation in the next project and the one after that. *The Q-Loop* provides an effective vehicle upon which to embark on a journey that demands patience, candor, and endurance."

—Drew Lawton, senior managing director,
New York Life Investments, LLC

"*The Q-Loop* treats the management of organizational change in a new and powerful way. It concentrates on the often overlooked requirement for vitalizing the organization to see the need for the change and to become enthusiastic about the future offered by it."

—David J. BenDaniel, PhD, Don and Margi Berens Professor of Entrepreneurship; Professor of Management, Johnson Graduate School of Management at Cornell University

"If you are in a leadership role in any organization, *The Q-Loop* is a must-read to drive your business and team to cultivate a strong culture of creativity and adaptability. More than just great guidance and insights, the book is presented in a very user-friendly, interactive style that enables you to immediately apply Q-Loop's valuable concepts into your organization – a start down the road toward a successful and lasting positive transformation. As a bonus, it's also thoroughly enjoyable and fun to read!"

—Janet Tsai Dargan, EVP, Strategy and Operations,
Sony Pictures Television

"A must-read for anyone interested in delivering enterprise-wide change. *The Q-Loop* is a unique yet highly pragmatic approach for crafting solutions that are actionable, achievable, and sustainable. We have used the approach in our portfolio companies with great success."

—Neal Pomroy, partner and managing director,
DLJ Merchant Banking

THE
Q-LOOP

THE
Q-LOOP

THE ART AND SCIENCE

OF *LASTING*

CORPORATE CHANGE

BRIAN KLAPPER

First published by Bibliomotion, Inc.
33 Manchester Road
Brookline, MA 02446
Tel: 617-934-2427
www.bibliomotion.com

Printed in the United States of America

Library of Congress Cataloging-in-Publication Data

Klapper, Brian.
    The Q-loop : the art and science of lasting corporate change / Brian Klapper.
       pages   cm
    Includes bibliographical references and index.
    ISBN 978-1-937134-52-5 (hardcover : alk. paper) — ISBN 978-1-937134-53-2 (ebook : alk. paper) — ISBN 978-1-937134-54-9 (enhanced ebook : alk. paper)
    1. Organizational change.   2. Employee motivation.   3. Leadership.
I. Title.
    HD58.8.K564 2013
    658.4'06—dc23
                              2012050832

For my family

CONTENTS

FOREWORD

Another book on corporate change? I can't deny that question ran through my thoughts when Brian Klapper, founder of The Klapper Institute, told me he was authoring a book on the topic, called *The Q-Loop*. It didn't take more than a second, though, to remember whom I was talking to—and to realize why this book would be so different from the rest. That's because Brian is unique. And so is his Q-Loop approach. In fact, it's positively revolutionary.

As former senior vice president and CFO of The Hartford's Wealth Management business and former Senior Managing Director and CFO at New York Life Investment Management, I experienced first-hand the way the Q-Loop delivers rapid-fire, permanent results. At The Hartford, we had tried a variety of other approaches, but when Brian entered the scene, everything changed. His expertise, passion, and distinctive approach inspired real transformation like we had never experienced. When I began work at New York Life, I had no question about whether Brian could help.

By that time, Brian had developed his one-of-a-kind Corporate Lab, designed by him along with visionaries from the MIT Media Lab. The Corporate Lab—two exciting, intense, and unbelievably rewarding days—got all of the participants to view our company and our approach to solving problems quite differently. He essentially provided us with a new set of lenses with which to view our business. Within days of The Corporate Lab, using the skills we learned, we kicked off an aggressive mandate involving a series of challenges that had eluded us for far too long. Because the ideas came from our associates, and not from an external consultant, the implementation spread like wildfire throughout the organization. Right away, we kicked off two more high-profile projects.

Our management team then wanted Brian to run more Labs, launching new projects. Each one was more successful than the last. In the end, the company took over and we were able to run the Lab ourselves as many times as we needed it. ROI for these expenses—multiples of what we paid. And it all seemed so shockingly simple!

Brian's methodology is unique. By engaging team members on a project from the outset, the team is immediately vested in meeting—and in most cases exceeding—targeted results. Using the Q-Loop's proven methodology with the expertise and buy-in from the teams, we were able to deliver truly outstanding results that were sustainable and that added tremendous value to our organization.

Simply put, the Q-Loop results in a grassroots mindset shift to embrace and execute high-level strategy. It creates cross-department alignment and pull for a transformation agenda. The reason the Q-Loop works is because ideas come from the experts within the company, not from outside consultants. Whirlwind results then create a desire to do more projects. Each time, we saw real results in under 30 days—not months or years.

What's amazing is how closely and accurately this book captures Brian's ability to get to the heart of the matter—fast. Prior to reading the book, I was skeptical that Brian could ever capture the depth and complexity of the Corporate Lab and the entire Q-Loop experience. He did it! This book truly reproduces the transformational process of the Q-Loop. With practical advice, lots of interesting facts, and actionable, hands-on methods, not only is this book the most helpful I've read on the topic, it's a darn captivating read from first page to last.

So while there are lots of books and approaches out there on this topic, Brian's is fundamentally different. I am so pleased that this process of moving from bold idea to strategic planning to rapid-fire prototyping to long-term implementation is available to anyone. For any organization serious about improving and sustaining long-term performance (and which one isn't?), I implore you to embrace *The Q-Loop*. Read it. Live its methods. Benefit from its guidance.

David Bedard, President
ING U.S. Annuities

ACKNOWLEDGMENTS

I wish to thank the following people for the roles (both large and small, real and imaginary) they played in helping me write this book: Jeff Bezos, who had this great idea for a virtual bookstore and who is providing one of the homes for my book; the Dean of Admissions at the Harvard Business School, whose rejection led me to Wharton, where I met my wife, Patricia; Patricia, your boundless love, perpetual kindness, and fierce intelligence make you an incredible partner and an even better wife; Mickey Mantle, for providing a role model for my Dad, who then became the role model for me; Bobby Murcer, for making me realize that I would likely never be the center fielder for the New York Yankees and had therefore better find a more suitable profession...and who made me weep uncontrollably when I learned he had been traded for Bobby Bonds. Every single one of my pre-med professors at Cornell who made it abundantly clear that I had a better chance of making it as a professional ballplayer than I did of succeeding in a career in medicine; my Mom, whose love and guidance have made me believe I would be successful in any career I pursued (but a doctor would have been nice too); Craig Lauer, for having the passion, talent, and drive to help me see this book through to completion; Lucy, Marti, and Gerard, for your unwavering support; Mr. Clancy, my tenth-grade chemistry teacher, who said, "Klapper, you could be insanely great...if you would only get your head out of your ass"; Joe Kulka, illustrator extraordinaire, who took scant wisps of ideas and brought them to life; Jill, Erika, and the rest of the team at Bibliomotion, for giving me the opportunity to write this book and allowing me the creative freedom to do it my way; Dr. Seuss, who inspired me to "Go Places"; my sister Fern, my angel, who is always in my heart; Thomas Friedman, who inspires me to keep preaching common sense although I sometimes get the feeling that nobody is listening; Thomas Paine, who has been called "a corset maker by trade, a journalist by profession, and a propagandist by inclination," which is something to which I aspire (except for the corset maker part); my daughter Alex, my son Josh, and my daughter Danielle—this book is every bit as much your accomplishment as it is mine because the three of you inspire me every second of every day.

PREFACE

The year was 1997. The meeting was the culmination of 365 days of work—fifteen hours a day, six days a week. I had recently become a partner in the Financial Services practice of Mercer Management Consulting (now Oliver Wyman), and was given the honor of working for the firm's largest client on the largest project in the history of the firm. Our task: "Tell us how to reinvent our company and rethink how we can shape our industry to win in the twenty-first century." As a strategy consultant, this mandate was as good as it gets—a blank slate, tremendous resources, and time.

We had more than thirty consultants putting out thousands of pages of analysis, running dozens of financial models, and doing hundreds of client interviews. As we finished our work, we presented our results to the CEO. Following the presentation, the CEO declared, "Congratulations to the team. This may be the most insightful, brilliant work I have ever seen."

At that point, he took the deck of papers, threw it against the wall of the conference room, and declared angrily, "I can barely understand half of the stuff in here! How are the hundred thousand people in my firm supposed to understand it? What do I do with this?"

One of my partners replied that there was an entire chapter devoted to the Gantt charts, which outlined roles and responsibilities, time lines, and activities.

The CEO replied, "I don't care about all that! What are we supposed to *do* with this?!"

Two days later I resigned.

I was professionally raised to believe that strategy consulting was the peak of the profession. Implementation was better left to those who did not make it as strategists. Boy, was I wrong. Following that meeting, I resolved to get out of the "grand ideas" business and get dirty in the trenches, where the real work is done, to help organizations implement. What I came to realize is that very few companies are effective at really getting things done. So I resolved to work with companies to fix that. Quite simply, I wanted to help companies get stuff done.

In 2005, I started The Klapper Institute (KI) to help clients execute transformative change. I had a lofty vision for the firm: to completely redefine the management-consulting industry. You see, I believe you are in the best position to solve your own complex business issues. You already have the answers—though you might not know it. KI guides you to uncover solutions from within your organization. You provide the resources for the work. That way, you feel ownership of the change initiative from the outset—and are able to maintain your reinvention after we leave. Our goal is always to build true client capabilities, so that our clients are self-sufficient within one year (and therefore no longer need our assistance). Finally, I believe strongly that clients should only pay for results with which they are "delighted." I love the word "delighted."

I wrote this book to help those of you who are not able to work with us directly. So many companies struggle with becoming great at execution, and because I can't work directly with all of you, I wanted to provide the formula for the work we do so you can do it yourself.

I had considerable fun writing this book. I hope the read delights you.

INTRODUCTION

What moves men of genius, or rather what inspires their work, is not new ideas, but their obsession with the idea that what has already been said is still not enough.

—EUGENE DELACROIX

I never did anything worth doing by accident, nor did any of my inventions come by accident; they came by work.

—THOMAS ALVA EDISON

Bookstore shelves are crowded with business books discussing change. On Amazon alone, there are more than eight thousand books on corporate change. So why do I think the world needs another book on the topic? Simple, really. Because a remarkable 70 percent of all change efforts fail to deliver their intended results, and because the phrase I hear more than any other from business leaders (despite having good people, great technology, and a sound strategy) is: "It's so hard to get anything done around here!"

Although some existing books on change are filled with interesting stories and rich concepts, they are just not specific enough for readers to use in their day-to-day jobs to truly effect change. This book, on the other hand, offers interactive content, meaningful examples of real problems and real solutions, actionable steps and suggestions, samples of what does and doesn't work, fresh insights, a new approach, and practical guidance for all types of organizations.

I won't claim that I can make transformational change easy. Believe me, it's one of the most challenging journeys an organization will ever take. But what I'll do in this book is share with you how to develop and implement high-quality ideas that are right for your company and then implement these ideas with a proven scientific method that is repeatable and sustainable.

Usually, when leaders begin a transformation initiative, they believe they have a clear understanding of the critical elements involved. Once they get partially into it, however, they're amazed at how difficult it is to get even the simplest idea properly executed. They then wish they'd known more before starting so they could have been better prepared. If they could have recognized difficult situations before they arose—or at the very least, before they escalated to the point where the initiative either ground to a halt or came off the rails—they could maybe have done something to clear the path.

Most approaches to change rely on the same basic tenets, which are incredibly intuitive but virtually impossible to deliver. The list usually goes like this: develop a vision, build a strategy, communicate the vision, establish a sense of urgency, generate buy-in.

It all makes perfect sense. After all, a leader would never have gotten the job without a clear vision. There's a tremendous amount of public data available to help develop a thoughtful strategy. Many effective communication models exist. And creating urgency is…. Well, it's this last one that's the problem. And solving it is a true art.

The single greatest challenge that prevents leaders from getting things done is their inability to generate buy-in for the change across the organization. There are thousands of books on leadership and even more on change management. So what makes this book different? *The Q-Loop* is a field guide, taken not from abstract, academic research but from the results of real-world lessons I've learned working with my many clients in the trenches for more than twenty years. Although most of my work has focused on Fortune 1000 companies, I have successfully applied these lessons to organizations that have anywhere from 160 to 160,000 employees—in the private sector, for government organizations, and within not-for-profit organizations throughout the world.

I'm now pleased to share my experience and insights with you.

What the Q-Loop Is All About

The Q-Loop is a process that forms a complete circle—from ideation to complete implementation. It's called the Q-Loop because, as the name suggests, it's more robust than a simple circle. Far from going in circles, like so many strategies intended to implement change, the Q-Loop works every time. That's because it relies on the real heroes in the trenches of your company, the ones who know how to get things done and to get people on board. Calling this process anything other than the Q-Loop simply wouldn't capture the full measure of this sweeping system.

When you look at the illustration of the Q on the cover of this book, you see that it shows lines before they enter into a loop. This represents new ideas and initiatives as they are considered throughout the entirety of your organization. The Q illustration then shows the loop itself, as these ideas and initiatives are delivered to upper management to assess and prioritize in relation to your overall business objectives. Then these ideas and initiatives are delivered back down to front line employees for refinement and a revolutionary new way of implementation. Finally, and this is perhaps the most exciting part, these initiatives are delivered out from the loop to the rest of your organization and embraced by the front line because the idea was initially created by them. Altogether, this process allows change to take root and flourish like never before.

Why the Q-Loop Works

It starts with a compelling story, one that originates with management but is written by employees. This approach enables employees to contribute mightily to the tale.

It also recognizes that employees are motivated by their impact on their customers, company, colleagues, and themselves, and it uses this motivation to help them lead the change. So instead of forcing the agenda on employees, the Q-Loop allows employees to drive the agenda.

It weaves together traditional problem-solving techniques using the scientific method and a constructionist element that lets employees dream and discover the art of the possible.

It teaches these newly motivated employees to take a mandate, validate and question it, and then develop a solution that they are excited to implement.

And it shows them how to do it again and again and again.

The most functional Q-Loop achieves the careful balance between intimate knowledge, organizational context, and the ability to direct resources. Specifically, the frontline employees have millions of contacts, translating into intimate knowledge of product, customer, and how the processes in the company really work. However, line employees often have a very focused knowledge base and limited, if any, ability to direct resources. By comparison, the executive suite has a tremendous ability to mobilize resources and great organizational context, but often limited intimate knowledge of specific products and customers and how operations really work.

Hence, a successful Q-Loop decision process is critically dependent on both the span of influence and the bottom-up input mechanisms that support the loop.

Keep in mind that the Q-Loop can be deployed at multiple levels within your organization to improve current operations, to create new products and services, and to capitalize on market opportunities. At the top of the organization, a large (or macro) Q-Loop spans many layers of the organization for processes such as strategic planning. A midsize Q-Loop is used for business process redesign and spans from frontline workers to senior executives. Multiple small Q-Loops can be used between frontline workers and department heads to create ideas for and to implement policy changes. This multitiered approach enables an organization to quickly mobilize Q-Loops to address specific projects and to pilot change.

Why Haven't Other Approaches Succeeded?

Likely, previous change efforts in your organization have failed for a number of reasons. They took too long, so your people got tired and lost interest. Or your other approaches failed to generate enough short-term wins to initiate momentum. Maybe your people couldn't take the time away from their day-to-day business to focus on the change effort fully. You weren't able to overcome the inherent pervasive resistance that runs rampant in your company (and all companies). You couldn't generate the huge amount of organizational energy needed to ignite and sustain a transformation agenda. Or you couldn't translate your change agenda into a motivating force for your employees.

Self-Diagnostic

Think of the last important project you were involved with. Now consider the following questions to evaluate the overall success of the project. The final grade you assign is likely an indicator of how most projects work within your organization.

- How long did it take? Was the duration longer than ideal?

  _____

- How many people were part of the effort? Was this number adequate?

  _____

- Were all necessary people identified up front as part of the team?

  _____

- How clear, quantitative, and focused was the mandate? Was there even a mandate?

  _____

- Was there consensus as to what needed to get done?

  _____

- Was there a formal kickoff to announce the project?

  _____

- How involved and supportive was senior management?

  _____

- What percentage of chosen team members' time was dedicated to the effort? Was this adequate?

  _____

- Were necessary adjustments made regarding team members' other duties to accommodate adequate focus on the project?

  _____

- How much time was spent in meetings rather than out in the field?

  _____

- Was the team fully supportive of the final recommendation?

  _____

- From the time the recommendation was made, how long did it take before implementation began? Did implementation even occur?

How would you grade the overall success of the project?

A   B   C   D   F

How the Book Is Organized

This book is divided into three sections to reflect the three primary sections of the Q-Loop. We call part 1 of the book "Maximize Your Organization's Collective IQ." This part discusses how your company enters the Q-Loop, addressing the need for companies to continually adapt and consider new ideas, as well as the need for your company to include *all* employees—particularly your frontline employees—in the idea-generation process.

Part 2 is called "Ignite a Grassroots Mind-Set Shift." This phase of going around the Q-Loop is the heart of the book, offering a revolutionary yet pragmatic method for pursuing and implementing high-value, multi-departmental change.

Part 3 helps you "Embed the Q-Loop in Your Organization." Unless change takes root and can be sustained long into the future as you exit the Q-Loop, it will be too ephemeral to be truly meaningful.

Together, these three parts truly offer for the first time the complete art and science of producing lasting change. The concepts in this book are ones that I have come to believe are essential for change—including capitalizing on your organization's collective IQ, looking to the front line for ideas and buy-in, embracing a formal process for change that's tied to a shift in the cultural attitudes of the organization, and learning to energize employees organization-wide by enabling them to think like owners. I've never seen another book quite like this one, so I knew it was the right time to create it.

Don't Play Nice with This Book

I invite you to engage with this book vigorously. Use a highlighter. Underline parts that resonate with you. Jot down ideas and insights of your own. Dog-ear the pages. Use Post-its. Talk back to it in any way you see fit, and have fun with it. And above all, try its methods. They can build a bridge between good enough and exceptional.

PART 1

. . . .

ENTERING THE Q-LOOP

MAXIMIZING YOUR
ORGANIZATION'S COLLECTIVE IQ

1

Adapt or Atrophy

Art begins with resistance—at the point where resistance is overcome. No human masterpiece has ever been created without great labor.

—ANDRÉ GIDE

It is not the strongest of species that survives, nor the most intelligent that survives. It is the one most adaptable to change.

—CHARLES DARWIN

In 1917, *Forbes* published its first list of the one hundred most valuable companies. Here we are, almost a century later, and only fifteen of those companies still exist (with several of them struggling mightily to endure troubled conditions). One company, U.S. Steel, which in 1917 towered above the other hundred companies, with three times the holdings of the second company on the list, today has an adjusted value just one-fifth of its 1917 value. True, it has entered its second century of doing business, an impressive accomplishment, whereas eighty-five of the one hundred were acquired, went bankrupt, or otherwise sank to the bottom of the corporate sea. Still, U.S. Steel's once tremendous might has ebbed, as it employs less than one-fifth the number of people it did in 1917.

Only one company, General Electric, has consistently outperformed the market for its more than 130-year history, its stock remaining one of the most highly valued in the world. According to Bill Rothschild, former

GE senior strategist, two of the five primary strategies that have led to the company's persistent success are *an ability to adapt* and *being proactive to the changing environment.*[1]

Adaptation is essential to healthy growth and economic vigor, and this axiom is more true in this second decade of this second millennium than it has ever been in history. An ability to embrace industry changes, technological advancements, and evolving customer demands opens up your organization to opportunities that your competitors fail to see. It's a chance to shed your skin and explore new and profitable innovations. It's how an organization thrives now and long into the future.

There is no question that today's business environment has grown into a rapidly changing whirlwind of fierce competition that has left many casualties in its wake. Customer expectations of products and services are escalating exponentially—in part because of digital technologies and more savvy, connected customers—and they are growing harder and harder to predict. Units of one, customized products and services, corporate transparency, and overnight fulfillment are now mainstream requirements. Governments are facing large and growing long-term fiscal imbalances and are reassessing and reprioritizing how they conduct business. Nonprofits are also facing huge challenges, ranging from a tighter economic squeeze that threatens programs and missions to stringent metrical proof of success expected by donors. Educational institutions, too, are being forced to contend with seismic upheaval, including technological changes, fiscal crises, increased competition, and much more.

To some organizations, these demands are stumbling blocks, even brick walls. To others, they are colossal opportunities. It depends on an organization's ability to recognize the possibilities, innovate, implement change, and sustain the transformation.

Ultimately, an organization's only chance for real and lasting success in this rapid-change environment is to be extremely nimble, flexible, and responsive to the constantly changing stimuli that impact what and how it develops, builds, and delivers products and services. Unless an organization is at the forefront of responding to change, it could easily be left in the dust.

Yet a paradox exists. While an overwhelming percentage of organizational leaders recognize the need to adapt, transformation rarely takes root in any lasting way. Why? And what can be done to convert this shocking rate of failure into overwhelming success for any astute organization that recognizes the necessity?

The challenge is to:

- Recognize the need for change and overcome fear of it
- Be scrupulously honest about your organization's current shortcomings
- Get everyone in the company to buy in to your vision for the future
- Offer the necessary tools to help deliver your vision
- Successfully coax a behemoth from where it is today to where it needs to be tomorrow

So Why Is Change So Hard?

If adaptation is a sign of a healthy organization poised to outpace its competitors, why aren't all change programs hungrily embraced and implemented with lasting success?

In my house, I'm always the first one up, out of bed by five o'clock in the

UNABLE TO ADAPT . . .

Blockbuster

In the year 2000, Blockbuster could have bought Netflix for $50 million—peanuts, considering Blockbuster's IPO in 1999 was $5 billion.[2] Since then, the video-rental chain has unnecessarily lost much of the value of its brand. Why? Inability to adapt quickly led this once ubiquitous chain to fail to keep up with videos by mail, dollar-a-night video vending machines, and videos immediately available via iTunes, Hulu, Amazon, and many others sites. A brand that could have evolved has instead filed for Chapter 11 bankruptcy, shuttered many of its locations, been acquired by Dish Network for $320 million,[3] and faces an uncertain future.

Eastman Kodak

For almost one hundred years, Kodak and cameras were practically synonymous, with the company controlling up to 90 percent of the North American market share.[4] Then came digital photography, at-home printing, online picture sharing, fun apps, and other trends that consumers love. Kodak's stock peaked in 1997. Fifteen years later, it was down over 80 percent.[5] It's not that Kodak didn't see or understand these trends—in fact, the first digital camera was invented and built by a Kodak engineer. The company simply wasn't able to adapt to these unstoppable changes and profit from them.

Sony

Enjoy your jog this morning listening to your Sony Walkman? Of course not. In the 1980s, the Walkman was as hot as the iPod has been for the past decade. Sony also dominated the market for TVs, video recorders, and other consumer electronics. Then along came more adaptable competitors like Apple, LG, Samsung, and other companies that responded to consumer wishes and evolving technologies. The result? Sony still succeeds in some spheres, but it lost big in others.

Research in Motion

Adored by hordes—especially businesspeople—BlackBerry was once the top smartphone. Lately, though, BlackBerry is withering on the vine. Arrogance, poor management, quality issues, outages (just as the iPhone 4S went on sale, no less), and lack of innovation have led to plummeting stock prices and dwindling sales. The potential to dominate the consumer electronics market was in the palm of RIM's hand—literally—but was handed off to Apple, Google, Samsung, and other more adroit companies.

ABLE TO ADAPT . . .

DuPont

In 1802, DuPont made gunpowder. From there, it expanded into dynamite and other explosives. The company went on to invest in the early auto industry, moved into materials science, produced many of the raw materials for World War II, and was crucial to the U.S. space program.[6] Today, DuPont is a veritable compendium of brand names, including Teflon, Kevlar, Mylar, Nylon, and Lycra, to name just a tiny percentage.[7] Like other companies poised for centuries-long success, DuPont is agile enough to fulfill its potential by persistently embracing change.

Apple

Single-handedly changing the music industry; redefining the way computers, phones, and tablets fit into our lives; and rewriting the rules of brand marketing, Apple is a company with innovations that can't be overstated. And these innovations are the reason the company's profits nearly doubled in 2012. Yet it's had failures. Remember the Newton? Another underperforming product was the QuickTake, the first consumer digital camera that connected to a home computer, introduced by Apple in 1994. Both were consumer flops. Yet these "failed" products were revolutionary, and were indicators of a healthy company aggressively pursuing innovation and risking failure.

Capital One

Capital One is unique. And it didn't become that way by accident. Embedded in the company by careful design is a culture that not only embraces change but requires it, measures it, and rewards it. Each year, Capital One creates and tests as many as fifty thousand new ideas.[8] Remaining focused on the future, the company considers change to be a core element of its identity. When dealing with a number that high, there are bound to be failures. More importantly, there will assuredly be profitable successes.

Nokia

From paper to power and from cables to car phones, Nokia has spearheaded many industries and trends. Founded in 1865 in Finland, the company has today established itself as a leader in telecommunications technology. As of the writing of this book, it is the second-largest cell phone manufacturer in the world, recently bumped down one notch by Samsung, ending Nokia's unprecedented fourteen-year reign.[9] At a crossroads, the company has a heritage of bold adaptation that will likely keep it moving forward instead of standing still.

morning. The same is true on weekends. But on Saturdays and Sundays, my early morning hours are spent a bit differently. I take a run and then pour myself a cup of coffee while the rest of my family sleeps. I sip my coffee on the couch while my Bernese Mountain dog, Yodel (who thinks he's a lap dog) climbs on top of me as I read *The New York Times* and any other periodicals I didn't get to during the week. This peaceful time before the rest of my family wakes is my well-worn pattern, my routine. My wife says it's become part of my DNA, and I resist any changes to it. If a weekend day begins differently, which it sometimes must, it doesn't feel right.

We all fall into routines of our own. Sometimes they're healthy ones, like going to the gym after work. Other times, they're less than ideal.

Organizations are no different, developing their own unique DNA. Years of patterns lead to ingrained and deeply entrenched sets of beliefs and behaviors that extend far beyond the individual members of the organization and into practices that are systemic and cultural. Particularly for organizations that have been around for some time, this is a kind of defense, and an understandable one at that. After all, the fact that the organization has endured indicates that the culture works, right? Change is risky, because by definition it involves doing something unproven, something that hasn't yet been shown to work.

The result is that fear of failure is woven into the very fabric that forms many organizations' cultures, while stability is rewarded. It's a logical response. But is it a smart strategy, considering that the line between stable and stagnant is a slight and dangerous one?

And while larger, older companies with complex hierarchies, greater bureaucracy, and multiple business units are at a disadvantage when compared with smaller, younger, lighter-on-their-feet companies, small companies are not immune to inertia, fear, and opposition among employees. The need for accountability and predictability at both large and small companies often causes people to run away from radical experimentation (later in the book, we'll address experimentation in more detail).

> ### DID YOU KNOW?
>
> General Electric was founded by Thomas Edison who, in 1931, said, "I'd put my money on the sun and solar energy. What a source of power! I hope we don't have to wait until oil and coal run out before we tackle that."[10]

Formula for Failure
- $+$ Failure to see a need for change
- $+$ Belief that I know better
- $+$ Inertia
- $+$ Fear of losing job or power or control
- $+$ Comfort with status quo
- $+$ No involvement in designing solution
- $+$ Don't see what's in it for my peers, my customers, or me

---

- $=$ Inability to embrace change

Why Employees Resist Change

Employees resist change for lots or reasons. They might simply disagree with the change or the rationale it's based on. Or they might believe the change will be a fad. Or there might be deeper psychological factors, such as a fear of learning new skills or of losing authority, concern over becoming redundant, or resentment over increased hours. Or more than likely, they disagree with the change because they resolutely believe that they simply know better. And in many cases, they are correct.

Imagine a company that's been around for a while. Executive management announces a substantive operational change to employees. It begins next week and involves some restructuring of the company. It will offer a significant competitive advantage to the organization. During the meeting at which the initiative is announced, response seems positive, by which I mean most people nod and say little.

Then comes the kickoff. In little time, quiet resistance bubbles up here and there in the form of slight work slowdowns, subtle sabotage, and water-cooler whispering. Murmured gripes spread. Then come the open complaints, which begin to infect even those employees originally on board with the change. Executive management, and likely middle management too, respond by pushing the change down the chain of command even harder.

As a result, employees resist even more, and the initiative goes over budget, past deadline, and is either scrapped or implemented in a half-baked fashion. Most certainly, it leaves a bad taste in everyone's mouth for the next time a potentially positive change is considered. To management, employees end up seeming petulant. To employees, management seems dictatorial.

It's fascinating how often this happens, considering that everyone involved would have benefited from complete, on-time, on-budget implementation of the program, because it would have resulted in the continued health and growth of the company. So where does the process go off the track?

Obstacles in the Way of Success

- Employees are worried about the impact that the change will have on their jobs, an understandable fear.
- Employees feel slighted by the unintended message that's being sent to them: the way you are currently operating is wrong. For people proud of their work, this feels like a slap, when the intention is actually to improve their work environment.

> **DID YOU KNOW?**
>
> The scientific definition of resistance is "a force, such as friction, that operates opposite the direction of motion of a body and tends to prevent or slow down the body's motion."

- People naturally resist being changed and instead want to change on their own. Because employees weren't part of the idea-generation and decision-making process, they feel alienated from the initiative.
- Employees are already outrageously busy and don't have time to take on extra initiatives, especially when management fails to fully support the change program by balancing the workload of those involved.
- The benefits of the change program weren't explained clearly in terms of how it will help the business and employees, so the initiative doesn't receive adequate buy-in. Memos, meetings, and Power-Point presentations are insufficient.
- Management simply believes that their requests should be honored, respected, and carried out, and so learn the hard way that the result is a cunning and covert insurrection by frontline employees.
- Management doesn't supply all the necessary tools and training. They also don't seem to be living the change themselves.
- Decisions are carried out on a one-way street—from executive management down to employees—and so workers feel disenfranchised and resist.

The result of these feelings is what happens with more than two-thirds of all change initiatives: FAILURE! (Or, at best, limited success—which, too often, means the same thing.)

How Leaders Must Handle Resistance

I once worked with the leader of an industrial products company who committed himself to a major change effort and worked like crazy to create a thoughtful implementation plan. He put together a six-person implementation team that worked full time for three weeks, building a plan that included the major tasks, supporting activities, roles, responsibilities, time frames, required technology support, and key dependencies.

RESISTANT INDUSTRIES OPERATING PRINCIPLE #35
"We do not need or want lots of new ideas. We do not have enough time or resources to execute the ones already in the pipeline!"

During a town hall meeting, the leader declared to the organization, "The implementation plan is complete!" He then thanked me and my team at The Klapper Institute for our help in crafting the plan. I tried to explain to him that the "easy" part was complete, but that the most difficult part—energizing the organization to coalesce around the new structure—was still ahead of us. He bristled, stating, "The plan is so intuitive and well thought out, it will be a breeze to get everyone on board." He asked us to check back with him in nine months, "once the new organization is fully established."

Nine months later, we spoke with the executive team. Our fears were confirmed when they told us, "Basically, nothing has changed."

The same issues that they had faced before the plan—slow decision making, too many approvals and handoffs, lack of role clarity—remained firmly in place. One senior manager summed up the situation when he said, "The CEO's enthusiasm was admirable, but for those of us who have been around for a while, we knew from day one that this thing would never stick. You just need to nod and smile, keep your head down and your opinions to yourself, and it will all pass."

When the leader heard the opinions of his leadership team (after his fury passed), he came to terms with the knowledge that change is not simply creating a road map; it is about getting buy-in regarding the *need* for the journey. It is about painting a vivid and compelling picture of the future, getting consensus on the route to be taken, ensuring agreement on the timing, and hearing and overcoming concerns from all participants.

This story is not unique. For most change initiatives, lack of alignment among the leadership team is the primary cause of failure. Too often, factions occur and sides are taken. Or there is not complete commitment to the vision and path. As a result, the initiative becomes bogged down by lack of consensus and stalls.

Methods for Removing Obstacles

- Articulate a vision and develop a thorough plan that is easily understood. To do so, leadership must be fully immersed in the details of the plan and must not delegate this step.
- Ensure alignment through one-on-one meetings, group discussions, a thorough data review, and fact-based analysis of the issues. To quote one of my clients, "Far too many of our key decisions are made in a data-free environment."
- Establish for the organization and for all members of the organization appropriate expectations of what will happen, how all employees will fit in, and what can be achieved as a result of the change initiative.
- Create a genuine desire for change among the employees by rousing organizational energy, including collective motivation, enthusiasm, and intense commitment (more on this topic in upcoming chapters).
- Establish that the very top leaders, including the CEO, have passion for the change and also the ability to carry it out.
- Address both the behavioral and emotional components of change. Far too many change efforts focus solely on the tactical and operational aspects and neglect the human component.
- Get in the trenches to help and to model the desired mind-set and behaviors.

- Build a culture of innovative thinking that promotes the freedom to experiment and ignore red tape.
- Trigger a sense of optimism around the change initiative. Change is often viewed as negative, yet most participants in the programs I help orchestrate find it thrilling. According to one, the experience was "the most fun I have had in twenty years working for the company."
- Expect and plan for resistance by identifying where in the organization the resistance might come from and how the resistance might manifest itself.

These actions will align your leadership team so that they can set an example for all other members of your organization. The result will be far less resistance and more passionate buy-in among all employees.

To execute strategy successfully, it's essential that you take your organization's current cultural temperature. That way, you'll understand its collective attitude toward change—both its openness to change and its points of resistance. By doing so, you'll determine the specific hurdles that will stand in your way as well as the people you can lean on to keep you moving forward.

There are numerous methods for assessing an organization's readiness for change. In my experience, focus groups, small-group meetings with key influencers, and organization-wide employee surveys are most effective at deriving thorough and reliable results.

— DID YOU KNOW? —

PayPal was not founded as the online payment service it is today. PayPal was originally envisioned as a cryptography company, and only later became a way of transmitting money via PDAs. Only after much trial and error did PayPal emerge as the go-to online payment system of millions.[11]

At the outset of a change initiative, distribute the following survey to employees. To elicit the most honest responses, let employees know that all surveys will be kept confidential. Go ahead and take the survey yourself—right now—based on an upcoming or imagined change initiative at your organization, and estimate its chances for success. Imagine how different members of your organization might answer the questions differently.

After the survey is complete, add the numbers and compare the total to the ranges that appear in the results key after the survey. These assessments will offer you insight regarding the willingness to embrace change within your organization.

Readiness for Change Survey

Please respond to the following statements by circling the number that best describes your opinion.

1 = Strongly disagree
2 = Disagree
3 = Neutral opinion
4 = Agree
5 = Strongly agree

I am comfortable with the current operating environment.

1   2   3   4   5

I am fearful of uncertainty and the unknown at this organization.

1   2   3   4   5

Management has not clearly communicated the vision and reasons for this change.

1   2   3   4   5

I believe that this change is not needed.

1   2   3   4   5

I do not agree with the direction of this change.

1   2   3   4   5

My role in this change initiative has not been clearly communicated.

1   2   3   4   5

I believe this initiative is simply the flavor of the month and will go away like many past change initiatives.

1   2   3   4   5

I am concerned about the new processes, requirements, and technology that are part of this change.

| 1 | 2 | 3 | 4 | 5 |

I fear that I don't have the skills and experience needed to manage this change effectively.

| 1 | 2 | 3 | 4 | 5 |

I don't have time to deal with the new work required for this change.

| 1 | 2 | 3 | 4 | 5 |

I am worried that I will lose power and control as a result of this change.

| 1 | 2 | 3 | 4 | 5 |

I am worried that this change will result in me losing my job.

| 1 | 2 | 3 | 4 | 5 |

Results Key

Add the results of the survey and compare the total to the following.

48–60 = There is a high degree of resistance to the change initiative, indicating that failure is a probable outcome.

36–47 = There is some resistance to the change initiative that will pose significant obstacles and could lead to this change initiative failing.

25–35 = There is a small amount of resistance that should be addressed, but success is likely.

12–24 = There seems to be very little resistance to the change initiative and success is the probable outcome.

CHAPTER 1 TAKEAWAY

Today's business and economic environment requires organizations to adapt faster than ever.

Organizations that view the changing landscape as an opportunity instead of an impediment are in a stronger position than their competition.

Culture is a lagging, not a leading, indicator. Culture only changes when people change the way in which they work and how they relate to each other. Working on tangible projects can be a way to ignite these changes.

Employees oppose change for a variety of reasons, but leadership can overcome this inherent resistance by:

- Making the change MEANINGFUL
- Changing leadership BEHAVIOR
- Creating and sustaining URGENCY
- Releasing organizational ENERGY
- Holding everyone ACCOUNTABLE

COMING UP

In the next chapter, we'll explore the importance of injecting your organization with new ideas and consider the various sources that can generate them.

2

Ideas—The Lifeblood of an Organization

The artist is a receptacle for emotions that come from all over the place: from the sky, from the earth, from a scrap of paper, from a passing shape, from a spider's web.

—PABLO PICASSO

The best way to have a good idea is to have a lot of ideas.

—LINUS PAULING

Let's now consider those finicky and elusive sparks that ignite the many new products, services, refinements, and enhancements that we as consumers enjoy and demand at an increasing pace. These temperamental ideas are what give rise to the great actions, products, and services of our day, yet they are so often extinguished before they're ever given a chance.

Drawn on a napkin, hashed out over the fourteenth hole, or devised while eating junk food late at night in a college dorm room, great ideas are the rich deposit on which organizations are founded. And organizations flourish because of new ideas. Quite simply, if a company doesn't recognize the need for a constant infusion of creative thinking and fresh strategic concepts, then that company most certainly won't be willing to take the necessary steps toward lasting change. Good, bad, brilliant, even godawful, ideas propel a business to new heights. They distinguish an organization from the competition, delight customers, and reward stockholders. Without them, organizations languish.

In fact, a recent survey suggests that more than a third of CFOs believe that a lack of new ideas is the greatest barrier to their companies becoming more innovative. Compare that to fewer than a quarter blaming it on too much bureaucracy, a fifth saying it's because people are too busy, and fewer than a tenth saying it's ineffective leadership.[1]

On the road from ideation to realization, however, a lot can go wrong. While this book offers a complete and revolutionary system of introducing, implementing, and sustaining valuable change within an organization, transformation starts—always—with ideas.

Before we move on, ask yourself the following...

- Do you believe that idea generation is important to future growth?
- How many measures do you have that focus explicitly on idea generation (versus optimization)?
- Can you say as much about your company's idea-generation ability as you can about your company's operating efficiency?
- Does your company have any personal performance metrics related to idea generation?
- Does your organization systematically benchmark other companies on creativity and idea generation?
- Do you know how to build a quick, low-cost experiment to test a promising idea?
- Does your company regularly build rapid pilots prior to full implementation?

DID YOU KNOW?

Organizations use the word *innovation* so much that the meaning is becoming diluted. According to *The Wall Street Journal*, in just one three-month period in 2011 more than 250 books were published with the word *innovation* in the title. And quarterly and annual reports used the word 33,528 times in 2011, up 64 percent from five years earlier. Yet, in the same *WSJ* article, most executives admit that they don't have an effective innovation strategy in place.[2]

IDEAS IN ACTION

In my long professional relationship with Teresa Roche, vice president at Agilent Technologies, I've been impressed by her attitude toward innovative thinking. In fact, written into Agilent Technologies' company policy is the following: "Our competitive advantage is to become the leader in innovation, creativity, problem solving and organizational flexibility." It's a bold statement, and one the company backs up.

One of the ways Agilent makes this principle real is through a twice-yearly Agilent Leadership Survey, which includes evaluations of leaders' ability to learn and adapt, help others learn and adapt, and take measured risks. Agilent CEO Bill Sullivan strongly supports the idea that employees provide an excellent perspective regarding management and are really the ones who can tell you what's happening on a day-to-day basis in their work groups.

What makes this survey different from those at other organizations is that it focuses on a list of leadership behaviors that Agilent believes are critical. The organization's focus for this survey is "speed to opportunity," which means that it is serving its customers' needs better and faster than its competition by finding the opportunities in the marketplace and getting there quickly.

When I spoke about this topic with Liz Ambrogi, global education manager for Agilent Technologies, she said, "There's a short list of behaviors that we feel all managers need to embody in order to have a culture of speed to opportunity." She added, "We ask all of our employees—because serving our customer is part of everybody's job descriptions—whether they believe their leaders are living those values. It's a great vehicle to shine a light on what's important and to let employees judge whether or not leaders are truly creating this desirable culture."

In 2007, when Agilent first put this program into place, the organization rated around 65 percent in terms of exhibiting the kinds of behaviors the company was looking for. Now, it's at 87 percent and compares very favorably to competitor organizations based on industry-standard benchmarks.

Why Great Ideas Perish

Chances are good that at some point you've witnessed a great idea die a premature and ugly death. Why? You know the idea was a strong one (maybe it was even yours). You also know that this brainchild would have benefited the organization it was intended for in some small but positive— or big and hugely profitable—way. Yet it bought the farm, rusted away because no one could figure out how to implement it.

After this happens a number of times, those of us with great ideas start to give up. We ask, what's the point of suggesting an idea or even pondering potential improvements? Longtime employees learn to go with the

ORGANIZATIONS THAT PROMOTE CREATIVITY (EVEN IF THEY DON'T ALWAYS ACT ON IT)

3M

For many years, 15 percent of 3M employees' time was reserved for creative work. That, combined with frequent opportunities to tell others about their work, brought together a scientist who developed a lightly sticking adhesive—which he considered a failure because he was trying to develop a more effective glue—with a researcher looking for a way to keep slips of paper in place in his hymn book. The result? Post-it Notes.[3]

Google

Google encourages its software engineers to devote 20 percent of their time to creating and pursuing ideas for new and innovative products.[4] Impressively, 50 percent of Google's products emerge from that limited time, Gmail and Google News being well-known examples. The software engineers may not be as proud of Orkut, but this social media site also resulted from this creative time. New ideas are exposed to the market through the Google Labs website and are tested both inside and outside the company; this helps determine the success of new initiatives by gauging how much attention and resources they attract. Pilots that catch on are adopted, and those that don't are shut down. Notably, there have been recent news stories about creative employees leaving the company because they believe it has become too bureaucratic and slow to adopt their ideas, suggesting how hard it is—yet how essential—for large organizations to maintain the innovative spirit that made them successful in the first place.

Xerox PARC

In the 1970s, Xerox gave a group of very smart researchers at the Palo Alto Research Center approximately five years of absolute freedom and adequate funding to come up with ideas about the office of the future. They did their job well, inventing the graphical user interface, the computer mouse, the laser printer, and Ethernet networking.[5] Unfortunately, these innovations may serve as a cautionary tale about missing out on opportunities.

Capital One

Capital One has designed a structure for continuously identifying new ideas, as opposed to a more conventional structure in which every idea has to progress slowly upward through approval channels. At Capital One, power is determined not by position but by persuasion—the data, reasoning, and strength of the argument. In fact, it's entirely reasonable for a Capital One employee to disagree with the chief executive, while at other companies an employee who does this may not be employed for long.

Rubbermaid

To develop new products in a competitive marketplace, where speed to market is an essential attribute, Rubbermaid doesn't spend a lot of time market testing. According to Wolfgang Schmitt, Rubbermaid chairman and CEO, the company doesn't do a lot of market testing or laborious intellectualizing about product development.[6] Yet the company succeeds by making innovation a core value within the organization, and it has led Rubbermaid to be named a "Brand of the Century" by *Brand Marketing* magazine.[7]

BMW

Leading car manufacturer BMW has launched a Co-Creation Lab website, where car enthusiasts can share ideas and opinions about the future of cars. This website invites people to contribute ideas, which helps the company form deep relationships with users—not just BMW customers but potential customers and influencers. It also gives BMW valuable access to a more diverse pool of ideas and points of view at a very low cost. Because users contribute ideas as well as evaluate one another's ideas, the entire idea-generation process is streamlined for BMW decision makers, who can review the activity on the site and decide which ideas will enter the BMW pipeline.

Sonic Drive-In

Founded in 1953 as a single drive-in restaurant, Sonic Drive-In now has three thousand locations and a market capitalization of over $2 billion. When interviewed in September 2003 on the occasion of the company's fiftieth birthday, former president Pattye Moore recognized "partnership over employment, fun over big business, (and) field-based menu development over corporate" as key tenets of this success. Moore says the majority of new menu ideas come from franchisees, their crew members, and vendors. When she visits stores, she asks the workers what they fix themselves while on breaks. She's learned that "because they work in the stores all the time, they'll combine all sorts of things for drinks . . . a number of our different shake combinations come from the crew members." She credits vendors for Sonic's line of cream pie shakes, a franchisee for the chicken tortilla, and a customer for the breakfast pancake-on-a-stick. Because field-based idea generation is part of Sonic's culture, store managers, assistant managers, corporate staff, and vendors feel free to call Moore and leave her voice mail messages on new product ideas.[8]

flow, even if the flow is starting to stagnate. And when new employees join an organization like this, they quickly learn to keep their mouths shut and do what they're told. Nothing more.

From the front line to middle management to the C-suite, great ideas are too often kicked to the curb, sometimes intentionally out of fear, sometimes despite heroic attempts to actualize them, sometimes because there's a collective belief that the status quo is good enough.

There are other reasons, too, such as lack of action, too slow an implementation, and paralysis caused by waiting for a perfect idea instead of acting on a less-than-perfect one. In addition, research has shown that employees in a negative environment, who are focused primarily on looking out for themselves and constantly defending their own space, are less innovative.

No doubt, companies that squelch great ideas can succeed. They often creep along, even profitably. Take a look at the NYSE company listings for proof. There are *thousands* of such companies.

But are these companies thriving as much as possible in today's ultra-competitive, über-rapid environment? Will they remain viable against increased competition? Are they able to embrace the changes required in these fast-moving times to achieve *long-term stellar success*?

How Creative Is Your Work Environment?

Consider distributing the following survey to employees. To elicit the most honest responses, let employees know that all surveys will be kept confidential. Go ahead and take the survey yourself based on how you believe rank-and-file employees would respond. Imagine how different members of your organization might answer the questions. Be as honest as possible.

I've always been an idea guy.

New Formations, Better Formations, Potential Formations...

After the survey is complete, add the numbers and see where the total falls based on the results key that appears after the survey. This diagnostic will offer you insight regarding how employees view your organization's creativity quotient.

Creativity Survey

Please respond to the following statements by circling the number that best describes your opinion.

1 = Strongly disagree
2 = Disagree
3 = Neutral opinion
4 = Agree
5 = Strongly agree

I can ask questions without being made to feel stupid.

1   2   3   4   5

I have considerable influence regarding how to get things done.

1   2   3   4   5

New ways of doing things are rewarded.

1   2   3   4   5

I usually know the reward I will receive for a job well done.

1   2   3   4   5

We don't have too many oppressive rules to follow in the workplace.

1   2   3   4   5

I know the reasons for the rules around here.

1   2   3   4   5

People want to know what I think about things.

| 1 | 2 | 3 | 4 | 5 |

There have been a lot of changes here since I started with the organization.

| 1 | 2 | 3 | 4 | 5 |

I'm willing to take a chance and don't have to beg for forgiveness if I mess up.

| 1 | 2 | 3 | 4 | 5 |

My boss really cares about what I have to say.

| 1 | 2 | 3 | 4 | 5 |

I'm excited when I see fellow employees trying new ways of doing things.

| 1 | 2 | 3 | 4 | 5 |

There is a lot of healthy competition here.

| 1 | 2 | 3 | 4 | 5 |

My ideas are included in important organizational decisions.

| 1 | 2 | 3 | 4 | 5 |

Mistakes are accepted.

| 1 | 2 | 3 | 4 | 5 |

Work is fun.

| 1 | 2 | 3 | 4 | 5 |

Asking questions is encouraged (versus being expected to figure everything out on my own).

| 1 | 2 | 3 | 4 | 5 |

I am not always under tremendous pressure to perform.

| 1 | 2 | 3 | 4 | 5 |

I have lots of freedom to get things done in the way I perceive to be most productive.

| 1 | 2 | 3 | 4 | 5 |

I feel as though I have a lot of freedom at work to do things my way.

1   2   3   4   5

Our culture doesn't subscribe to the notion that the boss is always right.

1   2   3   4   5

Results Key

Add the results of the survey and compare the total to the following.

81-100 = There is a high level of creativity at your organization. Employees believe that their ideas are listened to and so consider innovations and embrace others'.

61-80 = There is some creativity at your organization. Employees likely feel that their ideas are listened to and so it is worth their time to consider innovations and embrace others' ideas.

41-60 = There is a small amount of creativity at your organization, but employees likely spend little time considering innovations and do not embrace others' ideas because they often don't see the point.

20-40 = There seems to be very little creativity at your organization. Employees feel that there is almost no reason to ponder innovations or embrace others'.

Valuing Ideas to Create a Culture of Change

You've heard the justification (or some variation): "I've done it this way for the past ten years and it's always worked!" Or, "Don't fix it if it ain't broke!"

True, there's *some* merit to this belief. But just as often, if not more so, this belief—coupled with inaction—leaves you vulnerable to deadly attack by your more nimble competition or out in the cold as your fickle customers get what they want elsewhere. The landscape is shifting rapidly and lack of innovation can cast you out to sea before you even know it's happened. With the average lifespan of a large U.S. business now estimated to be between thirteen and fifteen years, there's little room today for standing still.

But organizations are running lean these days and, as a result, believe—accurately or not—that they don't have the time or resources. Workers are stretched to capacity and management is often faced with the daunting challenge of doing more with less. As a result, some leaders say they don't have the resources to devote to employees considering new ideas. They don't even have time to implement the ideas already in the pipeline. In fact, this is all the more reason to explore new ideas, initiatives, and opportunities.

Interestingly, star managers most frequently sought out for advice on new concepts often have the most negative attitudes toward change—partly because they have difficulty balancing new ideas with current priorities. Also, because they have found a way to succeed under the current conditions, new ideas might actually threaten the value they provide to the organization, an illogical response, to be sure, but one that is nonetheless the case in some organizations.

Often, the challenge is simply to recognize that there is a need to rise above the unquestioning acceptance of the status quo that exists in an overwhelming number of established corporate cultures, nonprofits, and educational institutions. Until people's implicit or explicit assumptions are challenged about how things within an organization have to work, they will continue to perform their duties as if they are wearing blinders.

Nurturing an Atmosphere of Creativity

Although organizations often consider creative thinking to be a luxury—and one they can't afford because of current pressures—my experience with many organizational teams confirms that anyone within the organization can generate great ideas. From executive management to frontline employees, fostering a culture of creativity and innovative thinking can be easier than you might think possible.

Let's consider the following five ways to shake the tree of ideas a lot harder than you currently do:

- Killing the status quo
- Altering your point of view
- Comparing your organization to others
- Imposing artificial limitation
- Looking for unorthodox opportunities

Killing the Status Quo

In the same way that people hold deep-seated beliefs, organizations have sets of accepted core convictions about how to get things done. Too often, these assumptions go unchallenged. The first step to killing the status quo is accepting that these core beliefs exist and then challenging each and every one. Such an undertaking will set you up for discovering and implementing new ideas ahead of the competition.

Consider Blockbuster's failure to recognize the changing video rental landscape, as described in chapter 1. If the company had challenged its long-held beliefs, it might have bought Netflix, though it would have been an unorthodox decision, just as Best Buy bought Geek Squad. At the time of the Geek Squad acquisition, it was considered foolish by many. But the $3 million purchase price was paid back hundreds of times over.[11]

In my own experience, I was once asked by Bank of America to implement its vision of "reinventing banking for the twenty-first century." The goal was to migrate from its current geographic-based business model to one that reconsidered the traditional branch format, focused on the customer as the center of all activity, and improved the experience of its customers.

To jump-start creativity in its people, the bank converted several local branches into "learning laboratories" that enabled Bank of America to quickly introduce new concepts, test them with live customers, and evaluate their performance. Hundreds of new ideas—from greeters to kiosks to play areas for children to informational videos—were introduced. These laboratories were transformative for the employees, who observed, interacted with customers, took lots of pictures, and later shared their observations with teammates in formal idea-evaluation sessions. By employing a learning laboratory concept, pressure to select the "one big idea" was greatly reduced and the fear of failure was eliminated. And seeing firsthand how the customer experience was transformed, bank employees relaxed their strongly held paradigms about which ideas would prove to be most successful. This transformation, in turn, drove them to ideate and implement a host of new customer experiences that they had never before considered.

Altering Your Point of View

To boost your creativity quotient, it's paramount that you break free of your existing point of view, which is easier to suggest—and even to intellectually understand—than to actually do. Compelling studies verify that people often refuse to jettison their deep-seated beliefs even when presented with evidence that overwhelmingly contradicts them.

To break stubborn obstructions that stand in the way of new modes of thinking, you sometimes need to experience something firsthand outside of the office or boardroom. Let me begin an example of this phenomenon with a personal anecdote. For my wife's most recent birthday, my children and I wanted to surprise her with a Mini Cooper. Because my wife manages our finances and I can't spend a nickel without her knowing about it, I needed subterfuge, so my salesperson drove the car to my house (with a large red bow on top), took care of the insurance and all paperwork, and let me pay for it two days after taking possession. He didn't even ask for a credit card. One week later, a beautiful box arrived for my wife with a welcome kit containing key chains, fun facts about the car, and several other goodies.

During this same time, in my professional life, I was asked by a leading insurance company to help reinvent the end-to-end customer experience for one of its rapidly growing product lines to produce a "game-changing level of customer delight."

RESISTANT INDUSTRIES OPERATING PRINCIPLE #18
"We are a great company. Our products are great. Our service is great. We need to keep operating in exactly the same way—but do it incredibly well—and we will be around forever!"

The experience my family had working with the Mini Cooper sales associate to build our customized experience was so memorably positive that I vividly recounted the Mini Cooper sales experience for the insurance team to let them experience for themselves what a game-changing customer experience really feels like.

The insurance company team was thoroughly inspired by the story and rethought its entire end-to-end sales and customer service process. A few members of the team even visited the dealership. They redesigned all of their collateral, created a beautiful follow-up box that contained interesting and important product and service information, added concierge-level customer service, and redrafted benefits about the product itself. Today, the offering stands out from the competition because of paradigm-shifting insights the team gained from an experience outside of the conference room.

Comparing Your Organization to Others

This approach can be a powerful driver of new ideas, particularly when you compare your organization to a seemingly unrelated one. As Steve Jobs once said, "Expose yourself to the best things humans have done and then try to bring those things into what you are doing." This strategy is not about emulating other organizations; it's about stimulating surprising ideas that you might not come up with otherwise.

Here's a brief exercise that uses this approach. Ask yourself, your leadership team, and all relevant stakeholders the following questions:

- How would Procter & Gamble expand our global business?
- How would Capital One generate insights and new offerings from our customer data?
- How might IBM reinvent our organization?

IBM began as the International Time Recording Company (ITR), and its major products were mechanical time recorders. In 1911, ITR merged with the Computing-Tabulating-Recording Company. The International Business Machines Corporation was finally born in 1924. By 1947, IBM was shifting to computers. Over subsequent decades, the artful changes to the company's powerful icon expressed the dynamic changes within the organization.[12]

- How might Coca-Cola expand our brand across new products in adjacent markets?
- How would McDonalds ensure a consistent customer experience globally?
- How would Amazon redesign our supply chain?
- How would FedEx redesign our logistics network?
- How would Southwest Airlines maintain our customer loyalty despite a turbulent economy?

These questions and many more—which you should now create—will prompt bold and improbable new ways of thinking. For a consumer products client who also want to created world-class customer service, we took a "field trip" to the Four Seasons Hotel in Philadelphia. The team inquired about having an event at the hotel and spoke with the hotel's entire team from facilities, catering, reservations, and concierge to experience the perfect customer service experience across several departments.

Imposing Artificial Limitations

It might be counterintuitive, but imposing limitations on your thinking can be an invaluable way to spark creativity. By constraining you, it paradoxically frees you to run wild within a smaller area. Imagine your organization limited by the following restrictions:

- You have to serve only one of your existing consumer segments
- You have to move from B2C to B2B or vice versa
- You have to slash the price of your product or service by a third
- Your biggest channel is now gone
- You have to double the price of your product or service
- You can't get a single new customer, so you must maximize value from existing customers
- You now can only interact with your customers online
- You have to partner with another company

I used a version of this strategy recently while working with a large asset-management firm seeking to build a fresh growth strategy. As an exercise, I encouraged the team to focus their thinking exclusively on their existing customer base. I asked, "If you weren't able to attract a single new customer, how could you meet your growth targets exclusively from current customers?"

The exercise forced team members to analyze the wallet share from their current customers. It also demanded that they segment their business not according to their traditional measures but to what extent their current customers were buying the company's full range of products and services. This analysis offered them two startling insights.

First, the asset-management firm had historically segmented its customers into large, medium, and small based on sales, and it rewarded sales executives based solely on customer size. When the team looked at share of wallet instead of sales, however, they realized that, while customer size was important, it was no more difficult to bring in a large account than a medium account—so size didn't necessarily correlate with effective selling. As a result, maximizing the value to clients by getting them to purchase a full suite of products and services was going unrecognized and unrewarded, and a new incentive system was installed.

The second insight dramatically affected the client's organizational structure. The client had organized its sales force geographically to focus on maximizing the relationship with the independent financial advisor community. This was standard industry practice. But when the team analyzed the data, several revelations emerged:

- The client was invited to submit a proposal for nearly every RFP submitted within its target market
- The financial advisor typically brought only one to two deals to the client, so maximizing the relationship did not serve to generate deal flow
- Despite making the final round for most proposal requests, the client only won 15 percent of the deals (the same close ratio of each of its largest competitors), so building a relationship with the financial advisor community was necessary but didn't result in increased sales

My client realized that to increase the close rate in what was believed to be a commodity industry, it needed to change its perspective. The firm decided to group clients by practice, develop practice leads, and focus sales associates not only on sales but on developing innovative industry trends and insights. It was a risky move, because it had never been done in the industry. But the result was dramatic. When my client's team made the final round in their sales presentations, they now distinguished themselves by the deep knowledge they had regarding trends, benchmarks, and insights. These insights convinced prospective clients that they really understood their business.

The following year, my client reached its annual sales goals...in March. And not long after that, one of its largest competitors announced that it was moving to a practice model.

Looking for Unorthodox Opportunities

To spur the ideation process, do not constrain your thinking only to improving products or services. Instead, rethink every touch point between you and your customers to improve how they currently interact with your organization. Perhaps you are forcing them to interact with you in a way that's less than ideal and you could improve it.

Boosting Creativity Among the Leadership Team

- Encourage as many nontraditional interactions as possible.
- Pretend you are a start-up that is competing with your organization. You have a limited budget but no operational constraints. How would you redesign your operations to put your company out of business?
- Purchase your own product or service—as a real consumer would—and record every touch point your customer experiences. Document all impressions, positive and negative, through photos and a journal that uses highly descriptive words.
- Purchase a similar product or service from several of your competitors and compare all touch points with those from your company.
- Track your company's and your competitor's online buzz, including reviews, comments, forums, and chats, and really listen to what the market is saying.
- Connect with your customers with specific questions that span the entirety of the customer experience.
- Observe and talk to real consumers in the places where they purchase and use your offering to see what alternatives consumers consider and how long they take to decide.

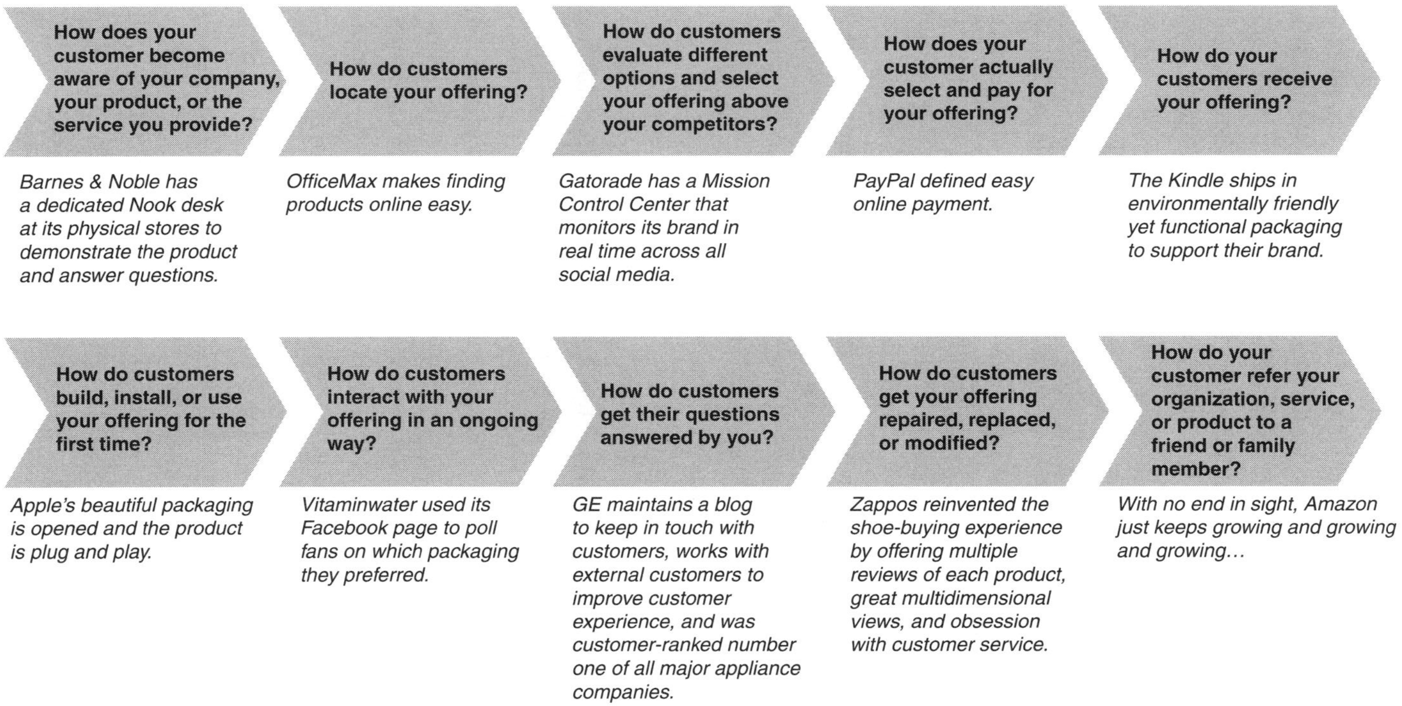

How does your customer become aware of your company, your product, or the service you provide?

Barnes & Noble has a dedicated Nook desk at its physical stores to demonstrate the product and answer questions.

How do customers locate your offering?

OfficeMax makes finding products online easy.

How do customers evaluate different options and select your offering above your competitors?

Gatorade has a Mission Control Center that monitors its brand in real time across all social media.

How does your customer actually select and pay for your offering?

PayPal defined easy online payment.

How do your customers receive your offering?

The Kindle ships in environmentally friendly yet functional packaging to support their brand.

How do customers build, install, or use your offering for the first time?

Apple's beautiful packaging is opened and the product is plug and play.

How do customers interact with your offering in an ongoing way?

Vitaminwater used its Facebook page to poll fans on which packaging they preferred.

How do customers get their questions answered by you?

GE maintains a blog to keep in touch with customers, works with external customers to improve customer experience, and was customer-ranked number one of all major appliance companies.

How do customers get your offering repaired, replaced, or modified?

Zappos reinvented the shoe-buying experience by offering multiple reviews of each product, great multidimensional views, and obsession with customer service.

How do your customer refer your organization, service, or product to a friend or family member?

With no end in sight, Amazon just keeps growing and growing and growing…

Figure 2-1: Content Creation to End User Flow Chart

Boosting Creativity Among Employees

- Hold a once-a-month lunch, introduce an "idea hour," or create small-team brainstorming sessions.
- Research and directly experience a competitor's products or services.

- Become a customer of your own product or service.
- Control the naysayers during ideation sessions.
- Welcome dissenting, unorthodox opinions.
- Implement an open-door policy to management.
- Allow face-to-face meetings.
- Develop an online version of a suggestion box, where employees can offer ideas and comment on each others'.
- Limit idea descriptions to a concrete twenty-five words (if an idea can't be stated succinctly, it may not be clearly conceived—yet).
- Do whatever is right for your company and brand.

When I think of creativity, I'm reminded of a story I heard from one of my favorite professors at Wharton, Dr. Ian MacMillan, or "Mac," as he preferred to be called. When Mac was a young entrepreneur, he started a travel agency that focused on highly specialized tours for groups seeking unique experiences. Mac took the advice of his buddies and invested some of the proceeds in Canadian timber land. When Mac finally went to survey the land, he found much of what he had purchased to be beautiful lakes. Now, beautiful lakes are terrific to look at but completely unproductive if you're looking to harvest timber.

So Mac had an idea. He would offer "Canadian getaway" tours to people seeking a respite from their hectic lives. But Mac had a problem. There was no shelter for these tourists, and spending a week without shelter in Northern Canada would be a bad idea.

Mac decided he needed to build log cabins around the lake. But that was quite expensive, so he put an ad in a travel magazine asking, "Are you man enough to find your own way up to Northern Canada and, using our plans, build a log cabin that you will use for your own shelter?"

Mac was flooded with requests—and within months, he had a small village of log cabins built by volunteers on his property.

As an aside, one woman came to his office and asked if she could participate. When Mac replied that the tour was only for "he men," she proceeded to lift his desk above her head and declared, "I'm a he man, too."

She participated.

Don't Overlook Your Customer's Ideas

There is a magical spot where your organization meets the people you serve. Whatever your product or service, whether you are a multibillion-dollar corporation, a private educational institution, or a government agency serving your community with a critical mission, customers are a tremendous source of ideas.

One way to coax these ideas from them is to simply ask for opinions around a focused theme; it's important to capture the ideas in a manageable way, without becoming overloaded by an unusable glut. Keep in mind that this deep resource must be controlled so as not to generate millions of ideas. Consider the approach taken by BMW's Co-Creation Lab website described on page 21, which encourages ideas, rewards contributors in intrinsic ways, and creates an efficient method for filtering the ideas to a controllable flow.

Customer ideas can result from contests and events, and, in fact, may not even need to be formally solicited. Many ideas happen as a by-product of monitoring what customers are saying across your social media. Whatever your method of collecting these ideas, customers will feel valued, particularly when given public credit and praise for the idea.

There are many compelling reasons to use customers as a source of ideas:

- You capture the buyer's point of view instead of the seller's
- Results tend to be practical
- It costs less than internal task forces
- Customer loyalty and satisfaction increase because people want to be listened to

Notably, many product and service innovations were sparked by customers, including Dell Linux systems, Starbucks lid stoppers, and Microsoft Kinex, to name just a few.

Social Media and Crowdsourcing

At the rate technology is changing, organizations are drawing on the power of mass collaboration to involve participation by more people than they could possibly employ. And that participation even extends beyond its customer base.

Related to customer ideation, crowdsourcing is not a new concept. The *Oxford English Dictionary* is one of the earliest examples. In 1857, an open invitation called for volunteers to index all the words in the English language, including examples for each and every one of the words' possible usages. OED editors received more than six million submissions over a period of seventy years.[14] A less successful example occurred in the wake of the BP Deepwater Horizon spill in the Gulf of Mexico. BP set up a call line to take cleanup suggestions. In one month, it received 92,000 responses, of which only 320 were categorized as promising, although the number implemented remains undisclosed.[15]

> **DID YOU KNOW?**
>
> More new information has been produced within the last thirty years than in the last five thousand and a weekday edition of *The New York Times* contains more information than the average person was likely to come across in a lifetime in seventeenth-century England.[16]

Crushing Bottlenecks

Most employees learn quickly that bureaucracy, hierarchy, and silos create bottlenecks for new ideas. To stimulate the flow of ideas, organizations need whatever information is relevant for solving a particular problem to be shared among teams laterally, in real time, irrespective of reporting channels and silos.

One way around bottlenecks is to intentionally create networks of managers charged with encouraging new ideas. This kind of decentralized team can identify promising new concepts and prioritize them so that they receive the attention they deserve.

Another way to sidestep the bottleneck of middle managers is to identify those who are interested in innovation and connect them in a decentralized network fashion. Their job can be to incubate ideas from cradle to grave. More specifically, they can be charged with generating ideas, prioritizing them, and nurturing them, all while being rewarded for success.

In addition, an organization can boost the number and quality of interactions likely to promote innovation if it creates the conditions that allow them to emerge.

Keep in mind that the vast majority of information, ideas, and knowledge within an organization runs through informal social networks, as opposed to official hierarchal and matrix structures. While command and control exerted by hierarchies helps a company to manage its routine processes and tasks efficiently, and formal structures help companies manage people, they don't help to cultivate and nurture ideas. Real work, including substantive innovation, frequently gets done along informal channels.

As a result, it's not uncommon to hear comments like, "If we need something done in a hurry, we go to Sally in the corner cubicle, not to my boss, who consults his colleague then sends word back down to Sally." In other words, instead of dealing with bureaucracy and delays, people choose to turn to those people who know how to get things done outside of formally approved channels.

Companies need to do more to leverage the power of informal networks, which are incredibly powerful yet difficult to manage because they are complex, often exist below the radar, and often are not repeatable, as people change roles or leave the organization.

Network mapping can be a useful mechanism to assess the span, depth, and influence of the network. It generally consists of four basic steps:

1. Scope the network.
The mapping can be performed on any size network, from a single department to an entire organization, and the time it takes to map is correlated to the network size, so it's important to determine the important group that would provide the most insight. Generally, networks that span multiple departments and cross several layers in the organization provide the most interesting results.

2. Conduct the survey.
The survey is generally focused on just a few key questions, for example, "From whom do you receive information to help you perform your job?"; "To whom do you turn for advice?"; and so on.

3. Analyze the survey results.

To complete the network map, it's important to receive a relatively high response rate (to ensure nobody is omitted) with a target range of 90 percent. Inducements may be necessary to increase response rate. Keeping the survey short and focused helps increase the number of responses.

4. Communicate the results.

The analysis of the survey is interesting. To make the mapping a useful tool, however, it's important to communicate the results throughout the network. Network mapping adds significant value by helping the company understand how business is *really* done, which can then be used to facilitate additional interactions and help drive transformation.

Rewarding Innovation

It is imperative that you begin to reward innovative thinking in meaningful, memorable ways. Through recognition and rewards, a healthy culture of competition may emerge. Create policies that support the open exchange of ideas and an organization-first state of mind, and one that ensures that ideas will not be ripped off or ridiculed.

Managers should construct incentives that stimulate collaboration by encouraging innovators to share their inventions and insights within the organization. There are two approaches to choose from to motivate and reward employees for their ideas, and both have their merits.

Intrinsic Motivation

An intrinsic reward is one that comes from within. It is an ideal trait in an employee in that it implies a sense of self-motivation. An employee's sense of intrinsic motivation can sometimes be enhanced with praise and added attention from management. Aligning an employee's values with the value behind a change initiative can also increase the likelihood that an employee will embrace the idea without added extrinsic inducements. If a person is interested in something, in other words, he will keep doing it even if it isn't being overtly rewarded by the organization.

Types of intrinsic motivators include:

- A sense of pride
- The excitement that comes from learning something new
- The delight in accomplishing something difficult
- Interest in overcoming a challenge or making an improvement
- A desire to be seen as cooperative

Extrinsic Motivation

An extrinsic reward comes from an external source. This sort of inducement can be powerful, but it can also be more short-lived than an intrinsic motivator. When an extrinsic motivation such as monetary reward is removed, so is the enticement. Intrinsic motivation, on the other hand, is harder to smother.

Types of extrinsic motivators include:

- Praise from managers
- A chance to lead projects or task forces
- Cash bonuses
- Increased pay
- Stock or stock options
- Not getting fired

Which of the above approaches do you think is more effective? Take a moment to ponder your answer before reading on . . . .

Now consider the fact that in Japan the average monetary reward for an employee's idea is $2.50, whereas in the United States it is $491.71.[17] Also, consider Daniel Pink's 2009 book, *Drive*, which presents a large amount of research implying that money can actually make people less motivated to be creative.[18] In addition, in my experience working on change initiatives with many clients, our teams regularly work 50 percent more during certain phases of the project—for no extra money—and they never complain. That's because the work we do is so exciting and rewarding, and promises a better future.

Are You Intrinsically or Extrinsically Motivated?

Consider distributing the following survey to employees. To elicit the most honest responses, let employees know that all surveys will be kept confidential. Go ahead and take the survey yourself. First, rate the statements honestly to evaluate your own motivators. Then, answer based on how you believe rank-and-file employees would respond. Imagine how different members of your organization might answer the questions differently to get a sense of what motivates people within your organization.

When you're finished, add up your responses and compare them to the results key that appears after the survey to gain more insight into whether your motivations (and those of other employees) are intrinsic or extrinsic.

Motivation Survey

Please respond to the following statements by circling the number that best describes your opinion.

1 = Strongly disagree
2 = Disagree
3 = Neutral opinion
4 = Agree
5 = Strongly agree

I think a lot about how my peers regard me and my work.

1   2   3   4   5

I do not enjoy difficult activities.

1   2   3   4   5

I want my superiors, colleagues, and subordinates to know that an idea was mine.

1   2   3   4   5

I hope that by suggesting a valuable idea, I will advance within the organization.

1   2   3   4   5

I put in little effort thinking about new ideas for the organization because I don't see what's in it for me.

1   2   3   4   5

I want to be compensated for coming up with a great idea with money, time off, or the like.

1   2   3   4   5

I embrace new ideas because I believe that my reputation within the organization is improved as a result.

1   2   3   4   5

I don't enjoy learning new things.

1   2   3   4   5

I am proud of my role at my organization because my peers and boss praise me.

1   2   3   4   5

I don't like figuring out for myself how to get something done in the best possible way.

1   2   3   4   5

When I perform an activity, I think about what my colleagues will say when I am finished.

1   2   3   4   5

I tend to watch the clock, thinking about when I can go home.

1   2   3   4   5

I don't like performing an activity unless other people know I'm doing it.

1   2   3   4   5

I like performing an activity more when my peers or boss tell me I'm good at it.

1   2   3   4   5

I don't feel any better as a result of performing an activity well.

1   2   3   4   5

Results Key

61–75 = You tend to be predominantly motivated by extrinsic factors, including financial compensation, increased praise, or a more valued position within the organization.

46–60 = You are more motivated by extrinsic factors, including financial compensation, increased praise, or a more valued position within the organization.

30–45 = You are more motivated by intrinsic factors and do not always require financial compensation, increased praise, or a more valued position within the organization (although they're nice to have).

15–29 = You tend to be predominantly motivated by intrinsic factors. You are self-motivated and enjoy doing new things and devising new ways to get things done. You do not always require financial compensation, increased praise, or a more valued position within the organization (although they're nice to have).

CHAPTER 2 TAKEAWAY

A lack of new ideas is the greatest barrier to organizations becoming more innovative. Without them, organizations languish.

Most organizations are running lean, so some leaders believe they don't have the resources to devote to employees considering new ideas, an attitude that needs to be eradicated.

Crowdsourcing and customer ideas should be used strategically.

Innovative thinking should be rewarded in meaningful, memorable ways, and not always with money, although recognition and rewards can enhance a healthy culture of competition.

Calculated risk needs to be a requirement within your organization to elicit bold thinking.

While not all ideas will be used, organizations need to crush an atmosphere where employees are fearful of sharing ideas, focus on looking out for themselves, and constantly defend their own space.

COMING UP

In the next chapter, we'll explore the importance of your organization's collective IQ and consider how it can be used to enhance idea generation and to contribute to more passionate buy-in for change initiatives from all employees.

3

Launch Your Employees on an Idea Quest

It's a pity one can't imagine what one can't compare to anything. Genius is an African who dreams up snow.

—VLADIMIR NABOKOV

Could we have entered into the mind of Sir Isaac Newton, and have traced all the steps by which he produced his great works, we might see nothing very extraordinary in the process.

—JOSEPH PRIESTLEY

Imagine for a moment an organization where people are highly productive, efficient, and creative...where they are empowered to share bold ideas, solve problems, and explore new opportunities...where they actively contribute in decision making and feel like owners in the organization's mission. Sound like a fantasy? Perhaps. But it's not out of reach.

Today, this description doesn't capture the current state of affairs at most organizations, where employees often feel left out of strategic decisions and overlooked in the shaping and planning of new initiatives once a decision is made to pursue them. When I set out to write this book, my singular and heartfelt goal was to enable organizations to passionately embrace change and to implement it swiftly and efficiently. Fundamental to this book is my unwavering belief that for widespread acceptance and adoption of a change initiative to occur, those living the change on a daily basis must fundamentally believe in it—and to believe in it, they must contribute by helping to shape it.

As president of The Klapper Institute, I have worked with organizations time and again to help them produce lasting change throughout the organization by leveraging the knowledge already present within their staff. Frontline employees—the customer service agents on the phone with customers, the health-care professionals interacting with patients, the cashiers behind the register, the salespeople walking the floor, the delivery drivers—are too often overlooked or not given a voice within an organization. Yet this group is closest to customers and to the products and services you offer. Without them, a change initiative doesn't stand a chance.

RESISTANT INDUSTRIES OPERATING PRINCIPLE #23
"Our senior management team has all the answers. That is why they are managers. Rank-and-file employees are so narrowly focused that it is too difficult for them to generate any meaningful ideas for the business."

According to a compelling survey, there's a good chance that you agree, given that 90 percent of organizational leaders believe that active employee engagement has a positive impact on success.[1] Chances are also good that you aren't doing anything about it, as this same survey reveals that 75 percent of leaders have no engagement plan in place. It's a massive shortcoming when you consider that a recent Gallup poll found that lost productivity resulting from disengaged employees costs the U.S. economy $370 billion each year.[2]

Your assistant, junior associate, bank teller, barista, pizza maker, custodian, or forklift operator might have answers to your organization's most pressing issues or fixes for time-wasting problems. These workers might have ideas for new ways to satisfy the customer or insight into how to tweak a pressing mandate so that this time it will actually be embraced by the rest of the organization. But most organizations won't benefit from these valuable IQ points because management doesn't invite meaningful, focused input and collaboration from frontline employees. Instead, they look elsewhere to unearth newer, faster, better, cheaper, more innovative ways of doing things, when the answer is actually right under their noses.

> **The challenge is to focus your employees' combined brainpower by asking smart questions and facilitating the flow of information along fruitful paths to solve problems and discover opportunities.**

Embracing Frontline Employees as the Real Experts

Frontline experts see a great many problems and opportunities that their managers don't. Depending on the position, a frontline worker gathers knowledge from perhaps hundreds of interactions a day. The tremendous opportunity for organizations is to pull this knowledge from employees' day-to-day experiences, make decisions, and act upon them through those same employees.

Interestingly, a win–win situation arises when companies look to their employees for ideas and when employees are asked to help shape management ideas and mandates.

Companies with high-performing idea systems report that roughly 80 percent of overall performance improvements come from frontline employees throughout the organization—while only 20 percent come from management-initiated projects.[4] Considering these facts, it's eye-opening that most organizations largely ignore the enormous resource of employee ideas. Either these managers don't realize the power of employee ideas, or they have never learned how to systematically capture and channel this wealth of insight to support the decisions made within the organization.

Without the passionate engagement of your front line, you will be at a

DID YOU KNOW?

Earle Dickson got lots of practice bandaging his wife's hand. Mrs. Dickson, an accident-prone cook, often burned and cut herself in the kitchen. Worried about his wife's safety while he was at work buying cotton for the Johnson & Johnson company, Earle fashioned a number of adhesive strips with gauze placed in the center and covered them with crinoline to keep them sterile. His boss saw the invention in 1921 and Band-Aids were born. Earle went on to become vice president of Johnson & Johnson.[3]

severe disadvantage. Tap into this powerhouse of great ideas, on the other hand, and you will unlock a vast and formidable resource—because when the front line sees strategies and decisions that result from their own astute input, they are substantially more engaged in making them successful.

A Brief Explanation of Collective IQ

Assume for a moment that an organization has a thousand workers and those workers have an average IQ of 110. The organization then has 110,000 IQ points available as a resource (1000 x 110). What percentage of this collective IQ effectively participates in market sensing and decision making? In most organizations, it's safe to assume less than 10 percent.

Clearly, not every brain within the organization has the same responsibility for decision making. Senior managers, after all, became senior leaders for a reason. Also, it's impractical to create an environment where all brains have equal relevance across the totality of decisions a company makes.

In many organizations today, however, decision making is concentrated in the hands of the people in corporate headquarters who are furthest away from the market—often failing to leverage a gold mine of information that could contribute to decision making and neglecting a wellspring of resources that would ensure solid execution of decisions made. Employees on the front line, in fact, are the first, and best, filter to the market and to product trends that they experience every day.

To gain the competitive edge from this heretofore untapped potential, you need to cultivate a culture in which staff at all levels can easily share solutions for improving the business. Empowered employees, after all, are more innovative and engaged because they have more of an emotional stake in the organization's overall success. Data from Madison Performance Group indicate that 70 percent of employees who feel actively engaged by management deeply understand how to meet customer needs, whereas only 13 percent of employees who feel disengaged know how to meet customer needs.[5]

When it comes to ideas, the biggest roadblock senior management often face is the widespread, deeply entrenched belief that ideas from the rank and file don't matter. Where did they get this idea? In many companies, this wellspring of valuable insight simply isn't encouraged, considered, or rewarded. Creating an infrastructure that changes this mind-set will foster an environment where your front-line workers are passionately engaged with your company's ongoing strategy of improvement. Open up the discussion to everyone. You might be surprised by who has the best ideas. You might also be shocked by how frontline employee participation lubricates the gears to get major change initiatives moving along smoothly.

> **DID YOU KNOW?**
>
> Icheon, South Korea, was at the top of the employee-ideas list in 2011. There, 620 employees submitted thirty-five thousand ideas, 95 percent of which were implemented successfully. At fifty-five implemented ideas per employee, the net savings per employee was close to U.S. $40,000.[6]

What Is Your Organization's Collective IQ?

Take the following survey to evaluate how effectively you tap into your organization's collective IQ. After you've completed the survey, add the numbers and see where the total falls based on the results key that appears after the survey.

Collective IQ Survey

Please respond to the following statements by circling the number that best describes your opinion.

1 = Strongly disagree
2 = Disagree
3 = Neutral opinion
4 = Agree
5 = Strongly agree

I sense that employees at my organization are frustrated or cynical because they aren't given the chance to offer input into the organization's future.

1   2   3   4   5

My organization leaves idea generation solely to senior management or an R&D team and doesn't seek input from groups that work directly with customers.

1   2   3   4   5

My organization has extracted all it can out of our current idea-generation engine.

| 1 | 2 | 3 | 4 | 5 |

When I mention employee-generated ideas to the senior management team, they dismiss the idea.

| 1 | 2 | 3 | 4 | 5 |

My organization's management team thinks it's too expensive to include frontline employees in cross-function innovation discussions.

| 1 | 2 | 3 | 4 | 5 |

Existing structural boundaries and management systems prevent people from different disciplines from efficiently contributing ideas.

| 1 | 2 | 3 | 4 | 5 |

Our hierarchy slows decision making and prevents employees from unleashing their full potential.

| 1 | 2 | 3 | 4 | 5 |

Senior management at my organization tends to think that frontline employees don't understand what's needed or that they are incapable of seeing the big picture.

| 1 | 2 | 3 | 4 | 5 |

In the past year, there were very few ideas implemented that came from frontline employees.

| 1 | 2 | 3 | 4 | 5 |

There is a long gap between when an idea is offered to when it is evaluated and feedback is provided.

| 1 | 2 | 3 | 4 | 5 |

We do not recognize and reward employees in meaningful ways for new ideas.

| 1 | 2 | 3 | 4 | 5 |

My organization is not willing to expend a significant amount of effort, time, or resources in searching for ideas.

| 1 | 2 | 3 | 4 | 5 |

My organization does not have an explicitly articulated expectation concerning idea generation when considering new hires.

| 1 | 2 | 3 | 4 | 5 |

We do not have an infrastructure in place to receive, develop, implement, recognize, and retain ideas.

| 1 | 2 | 3 | 4 | 5 |

My organization takes a long time to turn ideas into procedures.

| 1 | 2 | 3 | 4 | 5 |

Results Key

15–30 = You use a high percentage of your organization's available IQ. You have a means of collecting employee ideas and showing employees that their ideas are valued and used. Employees feel passionate about developing, collaborating, and sharing new ideas to improve the organization.

31–45 = You use a moderately high percentage of your organization's available IQ. You have some means of collecting employee ideas, although it could be improved. You often show employees that their ideas are valued and used. Your employees likely feel willing to develop, collaborate, and share new ideas when encouraged to do so.

46–60 = You use too little of your organization's available IQ and are missing out on significant opportunities as a result. Your employees likely feel that their ideas are not encouraged or valued and so they probably feel discouraged about offering new ones. The result of this frustration is significant resistance to ideas that come from senior management without employees being part of the ideation process.

61–75 = You use almost none of your organization's available IQ. Your employees most certainly feel that their ideas are not welcome or considered. The result of such a situation will be continued resistance to change initiatives that come from senior management, because employees are almost never part of the ideation process.

WHY ORGANIZATIONS SUFFER FROM LOW COLLECTIVE IQ

Employees guard their own territory

Fix by creating among employees a culture of trust, in which transparent communications and the open exchange of ideas are praised.

Team size is too large

Fix by reversing the trend of increased team sizes to improve collaboration among employees.

Employees don't know one another

Fix by creating meaningful ways for employees—who are sometimes from very different backgrounds—to socialize at and outside of work.

Departments don't interact

Fix by promoting meetings between department managers, and invite people from other departments to sit in on meetings to provide an outside perspective.

Executive management fails to set a good example

Fix by signaling a desire for collaboration with open floor plans, by asking for feedback from employees, and by making sure executives model successful collaboration.

Idea generation lacks incentive

Fix by tying bonuses and raises to real standards that demand and reward innovation and collaboration among employees.

Companies are increasingly global and partitioned

Fix by breaking down organizational silos by gathering teams of people from all levels, divisions, and locations who are committed to changing the way the organization operates.

ORGANIZATIONS STRIVING FOR A HIGH COLLECTIVE IQ

Toyota

The Toyota Suggestion System has been around for more than sixty years. The average number of suggestions submitted by each employee per year is close to fifty—about one suggestion per employee per week—and implementation is approximately 80 percent. Suggestions for improvement are prompted and rewarded by management and frontline supervisors. Using the evaluation factors of originality, implementation effort, cost savings, and level of the person making the suggestion, thousands of suggestions are efficiently considered each month.[7]

American Airlines

Legendary American Airlines CEO Robert Crandall had a unique approach. Every idea not acted on in 150 days was sent to him, and managers were often asked to defend why they were sitting on a potentially valuable idea, an unpleasant experience according to most managers.[8]

Clarion Hotel

In the services sector, Clarion Hotels in Nordic countries is distinguished by receiving about fifty ideas per employee each year. Compare that number to Sweden's average of 0.5 ideas per year. Clarion's method is a combination of idea coaches, brainstorming, and customer feedback. At staff meetings, solutions are developed to solve each specific problem.[9]

PricewaterhouseCoopers

Accounting and consulting firm PricewaterhouseCoopers introduced an idea-management website called iPlace to aggregate employee ideas that could cut costs, improve customer service, and increase revenues. Employees can easily post ideas, sometimes responding to "idea challenges." They can vote and comment on one another's ideas, and senior managers review ideas within thirty days and respond to the submitter.[10]

Bell Labs

In its day, Bell Labs was one of the most inventive companies in existence, its list of innovations too extensive to list. Chairman of the Board Mervin Kelly believed that physical proximity was essential. As a result, Bell Labs housed thinkers and doers in one physical location and mixed physicists, metallurgists, electrical engineers, and others to create both discord and harmony—and above all, radical breakthroughs.[11]

(continued)

Veterans Affairs

The VA created the Veterans Affairs Innovation Initiative, which allows employees to "help the department improve health care quality, access, and transparency in service to our nation's veterans." Receiving ideas from sixty-five hundred employees, the department selected a final seventeen that it is funding with $5 million. Though the percentage of ideas implemented is relatively small, the ones selected are considered to be extremely high value.[12]

Milliken & Company

Recognized for having two of the most technologically significant products of 2012, Milliken expects 110 ideas per person each year. This requirement is sometimes not an individual requirement but is instead part of the annual performance objectives of a work group.[13]

Dow Corning

Dow Corning uses a concept it calls the Innovation Index, which combines idea generation, employee participation, revenue growth, and patent filing to create a 100-point possible score. Developed with the CEO's full support, the Innovation Index is used to set targets, track performance, and seek out opportunities. The company evaluates the success of the Innovation Index by comparing historical data to figures from the program to demonstrate growth.[14]

RLI Insurance

The 291 employees at this relatively small insurance company came up with 1,319 new ideas in a single year. One employee developed forty-nine ideas, while another's ideas saved the company over $145,000.[15]

Idemitsu Group

Idemitsu generates more than 110 ideas from each employee each year. The company's Principles of Management may help explain why. The principles expect the company to:

- play a beneficial role in society by creating an environment where people trust each other and work together to realize through business the tremendous potential of human beings
- ensure that each employee develops into a reliable person and is respected in society, while upholding our vision and high ideals and engaging in mutual improvement through amicable competition
- attach great importance to our promises to customers and seek to be worthy of the trust vested in us by unfailingly fulfilling those promises.[16]

DID YOU KNOW?

When U.S. involvement in WWII seemed imminent, U.S. manufacturers needed to ramp up production, pronto. President Roosevelt launched Training Within Industries (TWI) to teach two million factory supervisors to generate and test ideas through hundreds of small experimental changes that could be implemented immediately if they worked. The result? Quality, cost, and speed improved an average of 25 percent, contributing mightily to the Allied victory. Although TWI vanished after the war, the approach followed MacArthur's occupation forces to Japan as the United States helped to rebuild the devastated nation. The approach became Japan's primary business method.[17]

Thinking Outside the Suggestion Box

Let me be absolutely clear: I am not recommending that you install a suggestion box and then sift through the high ratio of relatively low-value ideas in search of the one or two gems that can help to redefine your organization. I have worked in dozens of organizations that continue to use the age-old suggestion box as a means of generating ideas, and it rarely produces quality ideas. Why?

Far Too Many Suggestions

Typically, a well-promoted suggestion program will generate an initial influx of submissions. However, when there is no sense of the outcomes desired by senior management, the program becomes flooded with all kinds of ideas, most of which are completely irrelevant to the overall strategy of the organization. The person—and, yes, it is often a single person—responsible for reviewing the ideas can't possibly assess them in a timely or meaningful way, leaving those who submitted ideas to believe that their suggestions are being ignored, which is essentially true. As a result, employees surmise that submitting ideas is a waste of time because management does not value their opinions, and the flow of ideas stops—and employees are more discouraged than ever.

Too Many Irrelevant Ideas

Because most open-ended suggestion programs do not indicate the types of ideas that should be submitted, many submissions are irrelevant to current business needs and, as a result, must be rejected. A large number of rejections sends the message that, although management claims innovation is important, it's really not. After all, if they were interested in ideas, they wouldn't reject so many.

Too Many Redundant Ideas

When suggestion programs are not well defined, the organization will often receive the same ideas over and over. These are often inspired by common sources: town hall meetings, internal discussions, trade shows, and internal communications that tend to be widely seen by employees. Nevertheless, redundant ideas take time to review and they contribute to the problem of receiving too many suggestions.

Lack of Transparency and Recognition

Although some suggestion programs use technology that enables the submitter to track ideas, many programs operate as a black box with almost no feedback. So once an idea is submitted, it's never heard of again and the submitter does not receive credit for the idea. In fact, this was an issue at least as far back as 1895, when NCR employees complained that there was no good reason for giving ideas to their supervisors because the best ideas were stolen and the worst ideas sometimes resulted in employees being fired. In response, company CEO John Patterson implemented a concept he called the "hundred-headed brain," which allowed ideas to be captured and over 30 percent to be implemented.[18]

> **— DID YOU KNOW? —**
>
> The first suggestion program was likely implemented in Japan in 1721, when the eighth shogun, Yoshimuni Tokugawa, posted: "Make your idea known.... Rewards are given for ideas that are accepted."[19] In 1770, the British Navy allowed reprisal-free suggestions to be made to avoid the hangings resulting from ideas that contradicted a commanding officer. The first recorded physical suggestion box was used in 1880 at William Denny & Brothers Shipyard.[20]

Idea Quest

While there is software that tries to solve at least some of the problems listed above—such as vetting bad and redundant ideas—in many cases the

IDEAS IN ACTION

Intel employs a wide variety of innovation channels to discover game-changing ideas and unleash the creative potential of its global employee base of over 100,000. In a conversation I had with Kristi Plinski, director of global management and leadership development, she was enthusiastic to share with me a few of the organization's most compelling methods.

Every year, Intel employees are formally invited to share ideas that they want to see brought to life through the company's Technical Strategic Long-Range Plan (TSLRP) program, which has proven to be hugely successful. Along the lines of an Idea Quest, another effective method of allowing employees to share ideas at Intel are regular and frequent IdeaJams, a series of high-energy brainstorming sessions. In addition, CEO Paul Otellini and senior leaders conduct numerous webcasts and on-site face-to-face chats with employees (which typically are broadcast to the larger organization). During these sessions, people are encouraged to ask questions during the Q&A portion.

"Through these programs and others," says Plinski, "Intel gets thousands upon thousands of ideas each year, which are evaluated by a group to reduce the number to a manageable number. Then a review committee selects the final ideas."

Increasingly, the company allows employees to share and review one another's ideas through their internal social media, called Planet Blue, which helps the overall process.

Plinski adds, "Those employees and teams whose ideas are leveraged and pursued are rewarded in a variety of ways, including financially."

Compellingly, among Intel's core values are striving to "foster innovation and creative thinking, embrace change and challenge the status quo, [and] listen to all ideas and viewpoints." Clearly, being open and direct is a fundamental value at the organization, so much so that it offers a training session called Constructive Confrontation, which teaches productive ways for employees to speak their minds about important topics, constantly challenging the status quo.

result is merely a suggestion box 2.0 solution, which might be an improvement but it's not a solution. Instead, I have developed a better strategy that can be used in connection with other idea-generating processes to solicit the most fruitful, strategic, and relevant ideas from the collective intelligence of your organization. This approach uses another kind of IQ.

I call it Idea Quest.

The advantages of Idea Quest are numerous. First, it introduces a formal, disciplined process into what is often a helter-skelter, shotgun approach. That way, you reduce redundancy and rework by providing transparency and a one-direction approach. Next, it sharply improves organizational focus by recognizing an opportunity to be acted on and by quickly separating the best ideas from the worst so you can allocate resources effectively. It also increases the odds that the most promising ideas receive attention and the resources needed to implement them. Finally, Idea Quest lets you evaluate the effectiveness of the ideation process based on the number of ideas per employee or team, participation percentage, collaboration percentage (including collaboration among people who normally would not work together), time spent on ideation, and the number of cross-functional ideas submitted.

Let's now consider the four steps to an effective Idea Quest in more detail. Remember, these are ways to unearth great ideas. In the next part of the book, we'll explore a revolutionary new way to implement them.

1. Focus employees on a specific mandate
2. Engage employees in meaningful ways
3. Create an easy and transparent way to share ideas
4. Require that ideas be turned into a project plan
5. Evaluate each idea and respond promptly

> **DID YOU KNOW?**
>
> According to the Employee Involvement Association (EIA), employee suggestion programs have saved organizations more than $2 billion. EIA also reports the adoption rate of employee suggestions is 37 percent, indicating that employees are submitting high-quality suggestions.[21]

1. Focus Employees on a Specific Mandate

While open-ended innovation has its value, the most successful systems for ideation within an organization define focused business challenges, to encourage employees to solve specific problems—and to do it quickly. According to research, focused ideas are implemented thirty times more frequently than a suggestion-box approach that lacks ideation parameters.[22]

To use this approach, invite the appropriate employees and employee groups to generate ideas to address a specific business opportunity within a defined time frame. The invitation questions should look at a single opportunity and should be short, very specific, and highly focused. Here is a list of opportunities with accompanying invitations intended to concentrate employee ideation around the opportunities:

Opportunity	Invitation
We need to reduce the time required to respond to an RFP.	How might we reduce the time required to respond to an RFP?
Morale is declining across the organization due to too much stress.	What programs might we put in place to reduce stress throughout the organization?
This year, our organization is spending considerably more on overtime than we have in the past.	In what ways might we reduce our overtime spend?
Field turnover has increased significantly over the past year.	What types of initiatives might we employ to reduce employee turnover?

IBM uses this approach successfully, having launched an initiative in 2001 that it calls Innovation Jams. These Innovation Jams are online brainstorming and collaboration sessions designed to spark distinct innovation around a specific topic. By 2006, just five years after its launch, $100 million was granted to the top ideas generated by more than 150,000 IBM employees, family members, business partners, clients, and university researchers.[23]

2. Engage Employees in Meaningful Ways

Use multiple mechanisms to motivate employees to become involved in your Idea Quest. Successful methods include:

- Setting a good example by having management participate in contributing ideas
- Stressing the importance of creativity
- Ensuring that all employees know that you want to hear ideas from them
- Making sure that contributors share in the success of the result
- Encouraging all ideas through positive feedback
- Ensuring that all ideas are welcome
- Making it fun
  (See Boosting Creativity Among Employees on page 34 for more ideas.)

When I worked with Corning Consumer Products Company a number of years ago, I engaged company employees on a vexing issue. The company had been trying to develop innovative new uses for CorningWare. One of the primary drivers of the company's goal was that Corning needed to defray the enormous fixed cost tied up in its pyroceram glass operation. The most difficult part of the challenge was, paradoxically, CorningWare's tremendous success: it enjoyed a 98 percent brand awareness among female consumers and had an 82 percent household penetration.

I understood that the best way to solve the problem was to use company employees' collective IQ. A directive was given to the company's employees who were female and members of a racial or ethnic minority—from store cashiers to corporate executives—to consider how to make CorningWare products more attractive to underserved, high-growth-potential ethnic consumers (data revealed that female, ethnic-minority customers spent more on average for cookware than other groups). We used the engagement methods just listed and were overwhelmed by the great responses. Our Idea Quest was a huge success, resulting in profitable cookware designed to meet the unique needs of ethnic cooks, including rice warmers, paella pots, and large bowls for soup.

3. Create an Easy and Transparent Way to Share Ideas

Over a defined and reasonable time frame, Idea Quest participants should work independently or together in meaningful groups to develop ideas. The environment should be completely transparent to participants so everyone can see all submitted ideas, as well as ideas that are being formulated. That way, individuals and teams can build on ideas submitted by others. As a rule, there should be no negativity that can dampen the ideation process.

- Make sure that everyone understands that innovation is critical to keeping the organization competitive and that employees are an essential source of innovative ideas. (Note: it may be necessary to train employees in basic ideation methods, including brainstorming, mind mapping, and creative thinking.)
- Get people who do not normally work together to come together for this effort. This approach creates a dynamic that can spark unexpected ideas. Also, encourage employees to join teams in other departments to offer an outside perspective.
- Challenge the way people normally work. Encourage people to think differently and evaluate the issue from nontraditional perspectives.
- Create a safe environment where people don't feel they have to ask forgiveness.
- Encourage out-of-the-box thinking that challenges the status quo. Wild and crazy ideas should be welcomed.

Remember that creativity should always be rewarded, even if the idea does not wind up being implemented. A high volume of thoughtful ideas should also be rewarded for people really engaged in the process. Be sure that valuable ideas are implemented (more on this beginning in the next chapter), and publicize the process, the contributors, and the results to encourage future participation.

4. Require That Ideas Be Turned into a Project Plan

Without a workable written project plan, submitted ideas can be abstract and extremely hard to evaluate. An idea might seem sound, but scratch a little deeper and the shaky foundation is revealed.

By requiring that ideas be presented as a simplified project plan, weaker projects must be strengthened. Or they can be identified as weak more quickly and scrapped so that the stronger ideas can move forward. While a project plan doesn't need to be a full fifty-page business plan—far from it—key issues concerning competition, uniqueness, viability, and requirements should be considered and documented.

A basic project plan should consider at least the following:

- Overview of idea
- Business objectives
- Competitive advantage offered
- Degree of difficulty to implement
- Estimated time line
- Estimated cost
- Estimated revenue
- Estimated team size
- Brief risk assessment

5. Evaluate Each Idea and Respond Promptly

When ideas disappear into a black hole, contributors become discouraged. Allocating adequate resources for evaluation is important. An additional advantage of creating a transparent process (step 3) is that redundant ideas can be culled or combined to reduce effort.

To further simplify the evaluation of submitted ideas, an evaluation matrix that considers technical, market, financial, and operational elements should be used. This matrix should be completed for each idea and used to compare one idea to another. The advantage of using an evaluation matrix is that it allows decision makers to sort through potential ideas quickly by identifying their relative strengths and weaknesses.

		Alternatives					
		Option A		Option B		Option C	
Criteria	Weight	Rating	Score	Rating	Score	Rating	Score
C1							
C2							
C3							
Total							

Figure 3-1: Sample Evaluation Matrix

Evaluating the Effectiveness of an Idea Quest

To verify that the Idea Quest process leverages your organization's collective IQ, after you complete an Idea Quest, evaluate the process based on the following benchmarks. Specifically, you'll see a marked jump in the following:

- Number and monetary value of implemented ideas
- Number of ideas initiated
- Participation percentage of invitees
- Collaboration percentage of employees
- Overall amount of employee engagement, including the number of ideas per employee
- Average time from idea submission until implementation
- Number of cross-functional ideas submitted and implemented
- Number of collaborations among people who would not normally work together

Here's another challenge for you. On page 49, you took a survey that helped you evaluate the way you currently tap into your organization's collective IQ. After enacting the Idea Quest process at your organization, take the survey again and tally your score. I believe it will be substantially improved, specifically in the areas mentioned above.

Idea Quest in Action (Although Amazon Didn't Know It)

Amazon used the basic Idea Quest process when it created its new service, called Prime, though the company didn't call the process by that name.

In late 2004, Amazon introduced Prime, which was a huge success. After signing up for the service, Prime members increase their purchases on the site by about 150 percent, and the program may be responsible for as much as one-fifth of all U.S. Amazon sales. Analysts consider Prime to be the main reason Amazon's sales grew 30 percent during the recession while other retailers struggled.[24]

Prime was no accidental discovery. Instead, it was a result of the company employing the full capacity of its collective IQ, via an approach that is much like the Idea Quest process just described. Let me explain...

1. Focus employees on a specific mandate

For several years, Amazon was searching for the right loyalty program and asked employees to contribute ideas. The specific mandate was: create an effective loyalty program that will grow sales and increase customer retention.

2. Engage employees in meaningful ways

Throughout the organization, creativity and inventiveness are part of Amazon's culture. There were past examples of employees' ideas being implemented, so employees felt that their ideas were valued. Using a suggestion box feature on Amazon's internal website, an Amazon software engineer named Charlie Ward suggested the idea of a free shipping service.

3. Create a positive and transparent environment

The internal website was in place to capture many employee ideas. Employees knew that this particular mandate was an important one because it came from Amazon CEO Jeff Bezos himself. While the company could have had a traditional loyalty program up and running in no time, employees knew that the company was different and was looking for something truly groundbreaking, which energized them. The original idea was for a free shipping service, and this idea was applauded. Yet, through further consideration and analysis, company executives, including Bezos, transformed the idea into a flat-fee, two-day-shipping service for all you can buy, improving the original idea substantially from Amazon's point of view. In addition, Bing Gordon, an Amazon board member and venture capitalist, came up with the name Prime.[25]

4. Require that ideas be turned into a project plan

Okay, so Amazon skipped this Idea Quest step. But the company would have been even better off had it not! Writing a project plan for an idea points out the shortcomings and risks and pushes people to refine the idea into one that is even more meaningful.

5. Evaluate each idea and respond promptly

The pace from original suggestion to launch was brisk. Bezos commissioned Prime at an unconventional Saturday meeting in the boathouse behind his home, telling a small team of employees that they should appropriate company engineers and resources to get Prime ready for the company's fourth-quarter earnings report less than two months away.

Amazon Prime took a village to create—and in the end it helped to set Amazon apart from the pack.

CHAPTER 3 TAKEAWAY

You already have the answers latent within your company. The challenge is to tap into this powerhouse of great ideas.

Utilizing your organization's collective IQ is the most powerful force for real innovation and to fully engage your employees, making them more open to all change initiatives.

Identifying your company's real experts—especially on the front line—is a fundamental step to tapping your organization's collective IQ and persuading everyone to get on board.

Using the Idea Quest process will offer you a huge competitive advantage by letting you tap into your organization's collective IQ in a thoughtful and focused way.

COMING UP

We have come to the end of part 1 of the book. You are now about to embark on an epic journey in part 2—but one far more doable than you ever thought possible. You'll learn a repeatable and easily implementable new process that will let you turn your newfound wellspring of great ideas, creativity, and greater employee engagement into actions. It's the next phase of the Q-Loop.

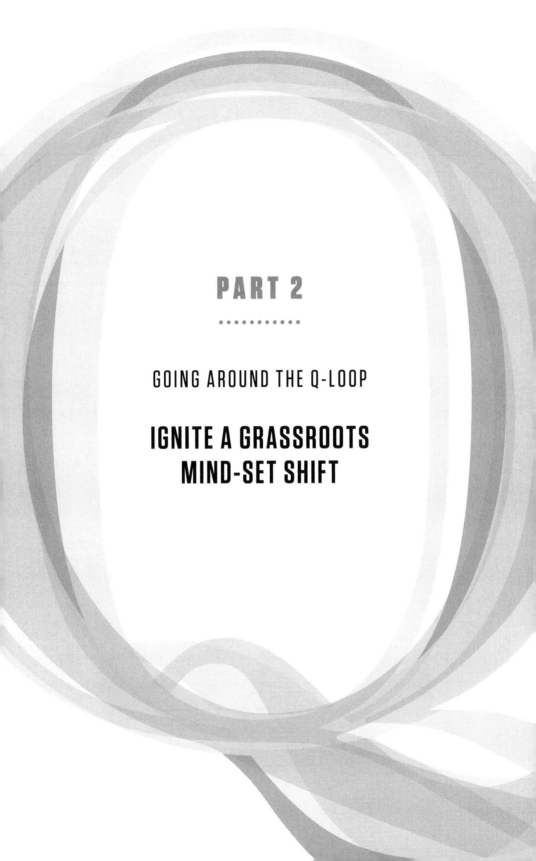

PART 2

. . . .

GOING AROUND THE Q-LOOP

IGNITE A GRASSROOTS MIND-SET SHIFT

4

Focus on a Mandate and
Form a Team of Heroes

A good poem is a contribution to reality. The world is never the same once a good poem has been added to it. A good poem helps to change the shape of the universe, helps to extend everyone's knowledge of himself and the world around him.

—DYLAN THOMAS

Never doubt that a small group of thoughtful, committed people can change the world. Indeed, it is the only thing that ever has.

—MARGARET MEAD

You've accomplished the first leg of the Q-Loop. Give yourself a big pat on the back—really, you're already a step ahead of a sizable portion of your competition in this regard. You've acknowledged the importance of continually adapting to the rapidly changing business landscape and to seeking out and considering new ideas. You've also accepted the need for your organization to include all employees—particularly your front-line employees—in an Idea Quest so that you extract and refine the best ideas from the collective IQ of your entire organization and so that every employee feels fully engaged with new change initiatives, regardless of the source.

It's a significant accomplishment and one that has prepared your organization for the next, and perhaps most critical, phase of the Q-Loop.

The three chapters in this second part of the book present a concept I first developed more than sixteen years ago and have been meticulously improving ever since as I worked with numerous diverse clients on a vast range of change initiatives. While no book could ever replace the relationships I share with my clients and the personalized experience I offer them and their organizations, I am about to share a process that has remained proprietary and, quite frankly, highly guarded for all that time. It is a process that has, without fail, delivered staggering results each and every time a client has employed it.

In the simplest terms, the next three chapters will show you how to implement a single, highly complex change initiative—yes, just one, but we'll get to how to repeat the process soon enough—and effectuate this initiative within just thirty days.

Perhaps it will be a new initiative, conceived after reading part 1 of the book. Possibly it will be one you attempted to implement before without success (this option is especially rewarding for me to witness, and I have many times). Maybe it will be something else altogether. Regardless, I will be delighted to participate—even peripherally—in the success of this initiative. And I do believe it will be successful.

In the end, if this one success is all the book offers, I believe that it will have been more than worth my time to write it and your time to read it. But this section of the book will do so much more. Chapter 4 will show you how to focus on a single change initiative and form just the right team to accomplish it. The following chapter, chapter 5, will take you on an unparalleled journey by which you will begin to see the outcome of the change initiative before the transformation occurs, which is precisely what will enable you to implement the mandate you choose. Chapter 6 will then show you how to take your radical new perspective and live out the experience by completing the change initiative project within thirty days—and fully implement the change inside of six months.

These next three chapters will guide us into the final section of the book, where you will discover how to fully embed this capability into your organization so that you can successfully repeat it over and over and over again. It's a truly wonderful thing to watch and will be an amazing thing for you to experience.

Let's get started.

How Successful Was Your Last Change Initiative?

Think of the last important change initiative you were involved with. Now consider the following survey to evaluate the overall success of the project. The final assessment is likely an indicator of how future projects will work within your organization.

Distribute the survey to employees. To elicit the most honest responses, tell employees that all surveys will be kept confidential. Go ahead and take the survey yourself—right now—based on a recent change initiative at your organization. Imagine how different members of your organization might answer the questions differently. After the survey is complete, add the numbers and compare the total to the ranges that appear in the results key after the survey.

Change Initiatives Survey

Please respond to the following statements by circling the number that best describes your opinion.

1 = Strongly disagree
2 = Disagree
3 = Neutral opinion
4 = Agree
5 = Strongly agree

Our last major change initiative did not take too long. In fact, it took just the right amount of time.

1   2   3   4   5

An adequate number of people were assigned to the team.

1   2   3   4   5

All necessary people were identified up front as part of the team.

1   2   3   4   5

We had a definite mandate, which was clear and had a goal that could be defined quantitatively.

1   2   3   4   5

We had consensus as to what needed to get done to accomplish our mandate.

I   2   3   4   5

We had a formal kickoff to announce the project.

I   2   3   4   5

Senior management was highly involved and fully supportive of our mandate and team.

I   2   3   4   5

We were supported to devote an adequate percentage of our time to focus on this effort.

I   2   3   4   5

All necessary adjustments were made regarding team members' other duties to accommodate adequate focus on the project.

I   2   3   4   5

We spent adequate time out in the field working on the project rather than meeting about the project.

I   2   3   4   5

When it came to our final recommendation, the team was fully supportive of it.

I   2   3   4   5

From the time the recommendation was made, implementation happened at a brisk pace.

I   2   3   4   5

Implementation was successful.

I   2   3   4   5

Results Key

Add the results of the survey and compare the total to the following.

50–65 = There seems to have been very little resistance to the previous change initiative. The outcome of this major change initiative indicates that employees embraced the change and your process was successful. Chances are good that the next change initiative you attempt to implement will also succeed.

35-49 = There was a small amount of resistance to your organization's previous major change initiative, but overall your organization implemented it with success. This resistance should be addressed, but success is the likely outcome to your next change initiative— although not without some degree of difficulty.

20-34 = There was a significant amount of resistance to your organization's previous major change initiative, and your organization struggled to implement it. It is likely that it wasn't implemented fully or efficiently. This resistance needs to be addressed if the next change initiative is to be successful.

13-19 = There seems to have been a high degree of resistance to the previous change initiative. The outcome of this previous major change initiative indicates that employees resisted the change and your process was unsuccessful. Chances are good that the next change initiative you attempt to implement will not be successful.

Moving Toward a Full Understanding of Solutions

Has your organization ever had to solve the same major business challenge more than once? Given the prevalence of this scenario in most organizations, the answer is probably yes. If so, why do you believe it happened?

I speculate that the process by which your organization solves its most pressing business challenges is inefficient. And, frankly, this is a best-case scenario. More likely, your organization falls into a scenario much more unfavorable and solves problems using an ineffective methodology. Don't be offended. You're like most busy, complex, overextended organizations, focused on the day-to-day activities that press in on you from all sides, internal and external.

Most organizations work in a similar fashion, with ideas typically coming from the minds of the analysts working on them or benchmarking what the competitors are doing. As discussed in chapter 3, what's so often missing is the deep knowledge that resides throughout the organization. Even the most interesting and thoughtful strategy will never be fully realized if it can't be embraced, loved, and championed by a critical mass. This lack of organization-wide support is often the cause of failure.

Employees are the conduit by which a company can systematically channel fragmented market knowledge into a decision-making process that results in better decisions and an organizational culture receptive to passionate execution. Organizations that have learned to maximize the collective IQ of their employees stand to gain substantial advantages, protecting and exploiting their relevance in today's market. What occurs in most organizations, however, is quite different.

In this matrix, you can see the range of possible approaches organizations have to solving problems. For a given problem, the x-axis represents the depth of understanding of "how" your actions directly contributed to solving the problem. The y-axis shows the level of understanding of "why" the problem occurs.

Problem-Solving Matrix

How much you understand the "how" and "why" of a problem determines the overall effectiveness of the chosen solution, as shown below.

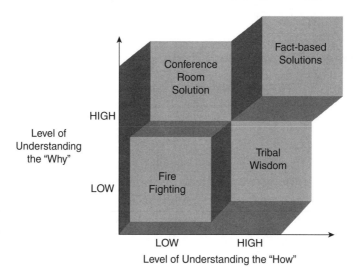

Figure 4-1: Problem-Solving Matrix

Firefighting

Organizations that solve problems without a thorough understanding of either "how" to definitely solve the problem or "why" the problem occurred must rely on firefighting. Firefighting is chaotic, frenetic, and reactionary.

As such, a tremendous amount of resources are consumed and the answer is often uncovered; however, it is highly inefficient and rarely produces an answer that will last over time.

Tribal Wisdom

Organizations that solve problems with a deep sense of how the organization was able to solve the problem but do not fully understand why the problem occurred generally rely on "tribal wisdom." Tribal wisdom depends on specific, generally undocumented knowledge from experts within the organization who are able to solve a specific problem but are often incapable of applying these insights to like problems across the organization. Tribal wisdom is also a relatively inefficient approach, as subject matter experts must be summoned whenever a problem arises. Also, an organization that relies on tribal wisdom is at risk because this deep reservoir of undocumented knowledge leaves the company every day at five o'clock.

Conference Room Solution

In my workshops and in many of my lectures, I use the phrase "conference room solution." It's a way to describe the far too common approach used by many organizations to solve their most challenging issues. The process looks something like this:

1. The senior management team becomes aware of a particularly challenging issue or business requirement.
2. The leaders gather in a conference room and proffer wisdom on how they solved this issue in the past or how it could definitively be solved now.
3. White smoke appears, followed by the ringing of the bells of Saint Peter's Basilica, which announces to the organization that a decision has been made.
4. The leaders form an implementation team, whose responsibility it is to execute the solution.
5. The team does its best with the resources and support given and ultimately reports that the solution has been implemented according to the specifications of the executive team.

6. One year later, a similar problem emerges and the process repeats, or this same problem once again rears its head, not having been fully embedded into the organization in an enduring way.

This approach is extremely common and, while often effective in the short term, does not produce lasting insights into the problem itself. So the organization tends to solve the same, or very similar, issues over and over again.

RESISTANT INDUSTRIES OPERATING PRINCIPLE #8

"It's better to have people work on 'extra' projects in their spare time. Instead of dedicating them for a short period of time on a new project, have them work for 1 – 2 hours per week for 6 – 9 months. There is simply too much 'day job' work to be done to allow for the luxury of dedication."

Moving Toward a Full Understanding

The problem with all of these solutions is obvious—simple even—but the causes are highly complex, deeply rooted, and have many tentacles reaching throughout the organization. Without the critical involvement of key employees and a clearly defined, properly supported mandate that is shaped by the frontline employees who will be living the change on a daily basis, failure is almost a foregone conclusion

Lastly, and regrettably, the least common approach to problem solving is fact-based solutions that rely on deep insight and analysis to solve the problem coupled with a deep understanding why the problem occurred. Once the how and the why are verified, root cause analysis can occur. And with root causes come meaningful insights that can be captured and applied across the organization in a once-and-done fashion.

Furthermore, fixing this problem doesn't require substantial capital investment to begin. Quite the contrary. Getting started simply requires that you identify the right idea to turn into a mandate and build the right team to achieve it.

IDEAS IN ACTION

In 1997, a century-old furniture company launched a home fur-nishings retail network of company-owned stores. The company believed it could dominate its market sector—if it could dramatically reduce the end-to-end cycle time (measured from the time some-one ordered a unit of furniture until it was delivered to his home). It needed to decrease the end-to-end cycle time from the industry-standard twelve to fourteen weeks down to four to seven weeks. Three years later, the senior vice president of the company got in touch with me to help the company achieve its still unmet mandate.

He took me on my first tour through one of the manufacturing facil-ities. Near the end he turned to me and, with real fervor, he asked me, "Do you think we can ever get it down to a forty-five-day cycle time?" I nodded.

Identifying a typical furniture group, we spent the next two days timing what we began to refer to as "buzz time," or the time when something was happening to the wood itself (it was either being rough cut, finish cut, assembled into doors or drawers, sanded, or finished). What we discovered was remarkable. End-to-end cycle time to produce and deliver a single piece of furniture was thirteen weeks and five days, but the buzz time was only two hours plus six hours for drying. So furniture production was really a single workday. The mystery was: What was going on for the other ninety-five days?

Noticing a piece of red tape on almost every piece of furniture, I asked the senior VP what it meant. He said, "Any piece with red tape needs a bit of touch-up, which causes it to be removed from the pro-duction line, placed in the cull hold, and fixed. Then it gets returned to production." I saw quite a few pieces of tape, so I asked him what his production yield was at quality inspection. When he told me 86 percent, I was skeptical. It seemed that more than 14 percent of the furniture had red tape.

Were they having a tough day? Were the pieces from a new col-lection, and all the kinks hadn't been worked out? Actually, he said, they had been making this particular suite of furniture for years.

"And you're at 86 percent perfect quality?"

He said, "Yes, at final inspection."

(continued)

How many inspection stations are there?

"Three," he said.

I suggested we run an experiment and ask every inspector except final quality assurance to take a break. During that time, the senior VP and I stood at final inspection and counted the number of pieces that had the small red tape affixed to the side. We counted a total 123 pieces, and every piece had red tape. Therefore the true first-pass inspection wasn't 86 percent, but 0 percent. By employing three different inspection stations, the company was, in essence, drowning out the voice of the process by providing a false sense of its production capabilities.

It shocked the entire organization to learn that, despite its hundred-year history, the first-pass production yield was 0 percent. We decided that before attacking the turnaround time, we would attempt to improve first-pass quality.

We assembled a five-person team of two plant engineers, a saw operator, an assembler, and a representative from the finishing room, all true experts in their area, and allowed them to experience The Corporate Lab, which will be detailed in chapter 5. Naming themselves the Red Tape Busters, this team's goal was to eliminate all red tape from the factory within thirty days.

The team analyzed all the defects that were being caught by the initial inspection team, which had never been analyzed because the deep analysis occurred after final inspection, and built a chart to categorize the defects. The team identified twelve categories of defects, ranging from dents in the wood panels (which occurred because the wood was stacked horizontally during transport rather than vertically) to glue that dripped out of the shelves (because the glue was applied to the female joint rather than the male joint).

Before you get the impression that these solutions were simple, I want to note that the team ended up going head to head with the CEO, who wasn't persuaded. To prove the validity of our findings, our team decided to commandeer an unused company factory on a Saturday morning and rearrange equipment to show the CEO our recommendations.

He was convinced. Within thirty days, the Red Tape Busters had identified and eliminated every category of defect, which enabled the furniture company to produce perfect first-pass quality. We then moved on to solve turnaround time.

Not surprising to me, all solutions were employee-generated and were obvious—but not until the team had the tools to discover them.

Getting Started

In many ways, these first steps to implementing a change initiative using the Q-Loop are the most important and riskiest part of the entire effort because they contain the greatest number of unknown elements. Don't be concerned, though. If the process for getting started is followed as out-lined below, the team should enjoy tremendous success.

1. Ensure senior management support
2. Choose the project
3. Select the project champion
4. Scope the work
5. Write the mandate
6. Select the coach
7. Select the team leader
8. Select the team members
9. Secure dedicated team space and team requirements

1. Ensure Senior Management Support

This first step is a preliminary one, and might seem like a no-brainer. It's not. Without the full support of senior management, the remaining steps are pointless. In addition to full senior management support, a single project champion must be identified. This is an important role throughout the project, and is particularly essential at the outset, when team members will feel most at sea.

Several years ago, a large financial services client asked me to help reduce by 25 percent both the time and cost required to prepare the annual enterprise-wide operating plan. The project was sponsored by the global CFO and, because it was company-wide, the finance function from all business units had to be represented. When we sent out the invitations to join the team, everyone accepted—except the global CFO and the CFOs for all the different business units.

When we inquired, we were told, "The global CFO does not attend such things," and "The CFOs have never actually been in a room together and really do not see the purpose of attending this type of event. Besides, they will each send a representative."

We responded to the client that, unfortunately, we could not begin until the sponsor and each of the CFOs was willing to participate. Because the project was as much about behavioral change as it was about operational change, not having management meant it was a nonstarter.

When the CFOs realized that their unintended but definite message was dooming the project from the start, they relented and everyone attended. The project was completed within thirty days and the team took 40 percent out of both the time and the cost to prepare the annual operating plan.

2. Choose the Project

This is an essential step, but not a particularly daunting one if you use the process outlined on the following page. This simple project evaluation tool can be a quick and easy way to help the management team evaluate several project candidates and determine which candidates present the organization with the greatest opportunity. Additional criteria can be added and all criteria can be weighted by their degree of importance.

After you score all potential projects, use a qualitative analysis to add a practical perspective to the scores. After these steps are complete, reorder the candidates based on their total score.

Before making a final decision, be sure to have a thorough discussion about resource availability and management support to ensure that the project can be effectively staffed. An understaffed or unsupported project can be doomed before it gets a fighting chance.

After performing this basic operational diagnostic, dive in. Change efforts will not work if the organization is always thinking about change, always planning to change, always meeting about change, always making PowerPoints documenting the change process, and rarely implementing.

3. Select the Project Champion

This role is critical. The project champion must be an executive who provides the vision for the team, reviews and supports its efforts, and acts as a team sponsor to the rest of the organization. The project champion must always have the authority for the entire operation in question and

Criteria	Rating					Total Score
	Yes				No	
	1	2	3	4	5	
The project is of high strategic importance to the organization						
The result will provide great customer benefit						
The result will provide high impact (quality, cost, time) to the organization						
The project can be completed within 30 days						
Once completed, the project can be fully implemented within 6 months						
The project fits within the strategic initiatives of the organization						
Resource Availability						
A cross-functional team of 5 to 7 top people can be made available						
IT resources can be made available as needed						
The project champion has the ability to commit time and resources						

Figure 4-2: Project Evaluation Matrix

is often—but not always—the process owner. The project champion's primary responsibilities are to:

- Maintain the overall responsibility, authority, and accountability for the effort
- Select and define the project mandate
- Select the team leader, coach, core team, and satellite team members
- Establish weekly commitment and project duration
- Ensure time commitment is maintained (communicate time commitment to management of team members; ensure appropriate backup resources are in place for duration of project; prevent team members from "double-jobbing"; make sure work-life balance for team members is maintained)

- Provide guidance, support, clarification, and direction throughout the course of the work
- Review progress and clear any obstacles that emerge during the project
- Ensure key stakeholders, especially those outside the sponsor's organization, have appropriate involvement
- Enable experiments designed by the team to achieve fast-track status to encourage rapid prototyping and rollout
- Implement the changes recommended by the team
- Meet with the team and feed lessons learned into a system that captures best practices for future team efforts
- Clear any obstacles that impede the team's progress

As you can see, it's no small task. So choose wisely.

4. Scope the Work

The project scope describes in detail the project's deliverables, the boundaries, and the work required to create those deliverables. You can think of project scope as a box. High-level scope defines the sides of the box and separates what is relevant to your project from that which is irrelevant.

This scope definition should be clear and understandable to all project stakeholders. It should adequately state the scope and limitations of the project, as well as its major goals or objectives. Once the project starts, you should not have a lot of requests to change boundaries and deliverables.

More specifically, the detailed project scope statement includes the following documents:

- Objectives: these should be measurable and observable project success criteria
- Scope description: this should adequately describe the qualities of the product, service, or deliverable
- Requirements: these prioritized requisites should detail the conditions or capabilities the project deliverables must have to comply with the expectations and standards of the client stated in an agreement or contract
- Boundaries: through this, the stakeholders are able to gauge whether a particular component is within the scope and limitation of the project

- Deliverables: includes the project outputs and the additional results of the project, such as documentations and reports, depending on the specifications in the project management scope statement

5. Write the Mandate

For any team to be successful, it must have a clearly defined sense of purpose. This purpose comes from a well-crafted mandate.

The mandate should unambiguously state your team's goals and why achievement of these goals is critical to the organization. The mandate needs to provide focus and should emphasize no more than two basic themes. It should also serve as a rallying cry and a basis for enthusiasm. Finally, the mandate should be brief, memorable, and in words meaningful to all members of the team. Think elevator pitch, not long-winded speech.

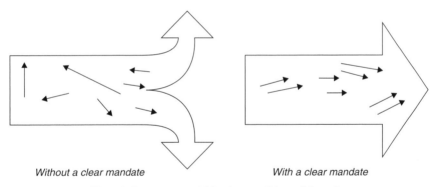

Without a clear mandate   With a clear mandate

Figure 4-3: The Advantage of Having a Clear Mandate

A well-crafted mandate provides the team with:

- A clear understanding of the problem
- Direct linkage between the organization's strategy and the mission for the team
- Key metrics related to the problem
- The expected time commitment for each of the team members
- A vision of how the sponsor defines success with clear, output-based goals

These output-based goals have five primary criteria. They are:

1. Specific—the more specific a goal is, the more likely it will motivate people to work toward it
2. Meaningful—the team must believe that their work will have a significant impact on the organization
3. Measurable—the mandate must make it easy to determine how well the task was achieved
4. Ambitious yet attainable—goals that are impossible to achieve will frustrate, not motivate, but if the bar is not raised high enough, the team will not move outside of their current paradigms to consider breakthrough solutions
5. Timely—the mandate should be appropriately focused to enable the team to achieve prototype results within thirty days

I have witnessed many excellent mandates, including the need to increase profitability of a service division, optimize the client-facing organizational structure, right-size the service offering across an organization, create a process that does not currently exist, and take cost or time out of a current process. Here are several more detailed examples:

- Develop a "game changing" customer service model that will enable the company to develop a reputation as the customer service leader.
- Improve sales force productivity by 30 percent for global sales operations.
- Accelerate the quarterly close from fifteenth business day to the tenth business day for the global business operations.
- Create a pull production assembly process that will result in a 50 percent improvement in first-pass quality (for the cabinet room) and a 50 percent improvement in case unit throughput (as measured by number of quality units assembled per person).
- Reduce the cycle time from 282 days to twenty-eight days for the end-to-end business acquisition process beginning with the identification of a prospect through the point of case installation. In order to achieve breakthrough results, we should eliminate all activities that do not benefit the customer or the company.
- Optimize IT procurement and deployment.

Reduce time to market for new hardware deployment by 20 percent for both pre-work component and post-receipt component

Maintain high levels of user satisfaction—e.g., newly deployed machine contains all the needed applications, services, and data needed by the user and in good working order

Reduce the time/cost to return old equipment to the leasing company by 20 percent

- Reduce the cost of client reporting.

Deliver client reports within five business days following month/quarter end

Maintain quality such that less than 1 percent of client reports require revision

Reduce overtime associated with producing client reports by 50 percent

- Allow underwriting team to provide additional sales and business development support, through increasing underwriting work efficiency by 30 percent (from RFP request through final sale).

6. Select the Coach

An ideal coach is someone who is experienced in working with teams and can efficiently and effectively guide the team through the project. The coach generally works behind the scenes with the project champion and team leader to support the team.

More specifically, the coach works with the team leader to determine the appropriate analytical pathway to ensure a timely and successful project. Most mandates fall into one of three categories: better, faster, or cheaper. In some cases, the mandates will combine elements of each. Regardless of the complexity of the mandate, it's vital that the coach recognize the likely range of solutions so she can guide the team toward the appropriate analysis needed to efficiently deliver its mandate. As Vince Lombardi was fond of saying, "The difference between [a good coach and an average coach] is to know what you want, and know what the end is supposed to look like. If a coach doesn't know what the end is supposed to look like, he won't know it when he sees it."[1]

The coach also works with the team leader prior to major meetings to ensure that the leader is capable and is comfortable running the meeting.

The coach should ensure that there is a sense of urgency, that team members are excited about the project, and that everyone feels free to experiment without worrying about reprisal. Additionally, the coach plans upcoming meetings, reviews agendas as necessary, and helps to structure the analysis.

Keep in mind that coaching is basically a series of conversations between a coach and an individual (or group) within a productive, results-oriented context. It involves assisting and encouraging individuals to access what they already know and is more about asking the right questions than providing answers. A coach works with the group to establish and clarify purpose and goals and develop a plan of action to achieve these goals.

Other duties include managing conflict, managing interpersonal relationships, dealing with team member difficulties, coordinating team activities, and addressing organizational difficulties outside of team scope that might affect the project.

> ### — DID YOU KNOW? —
>
> John Wooden, legendary UCLA basketball coach, developed what he called the Pyramid of Success. It's a useful selection and arrangement of the habits that are fundamental to his definition of success—which is, "peace of mind that is a direct result of self-satisfaction in knowing that you made the effort to become the best that you are capable of becoming."[2]

7. Select the Team Leader

The team leader is often—but not always—a manager or supervisor in the area where most of the change is likely to occur. The leader must be effective working in a team environment and have a reputation as a thought leader. The team leader cannot, however, be viewed as "the person with all of the answers," or the creativity of the team will morph into the ideas put forth solely by the team leader, and the other team members will not apply the necessary rigor to the work.

The team leader is charged with creating and maintaining an effective working environment and helping the team resolve its problems so that it can operate with maximum performance. This person schedules and generally runs most team meetings and also manages or delegates administrative details. Sharing in the team's work but also responsible for the quality of the work produced by team members, this person is responsible for overseeing analysis and preparation of reports and presentations. He also acts as a conduit to the project champion and coach and informs others in the organization who might be affected by the team's work.

Among the many desirable attributes of a team leader are:

People Skills

A good team leader:

- Possesses strong interpersonal skills, both with individuals as well as in groups
- Knows how to create consensus, build teams, resolve conflict, and provide timely feedback
- Can get results by working through others, not simply by working hard as an individual
- Has the ability to be facilitative or directive as the situation demands
- Is a well-respected influencer in the organization
- Maintains commitment and confidence of each team member, as well as the team as a whole

Technical Skills

The team leader:

- Understands and is capable of guiding a team through the use of the basic scientific tools, data-analysis techniques, and the scientific method
- Contributes equally to the real work performed by the team
- Is not afraid to volunteer for the difficult jobs that others on the team might avoid

Communication Skills

The leader of the team:

- Keeps the team purpose and approach in front of the team at all times
- Maintains a big-picture perspective, particularly when the team gets bogged down in the analysis
- Organizes and runs meetings efficiently and enthusiastically
- Effectively manages the relationships with the rest of the organization

- Works effectively through the sponsor
- Actively invites everyone to participate
- Is capable of moving the team from conflict to consensual decisions
- Communicates a persistently positive attitude toward the project

Project Management Skills

An effective team leader:

- Understands the problems, opportunities, and expectations of each team member's role
- Recognizes that project teams will have conflicts, but this is a natural part of group development
- Understands who the stakeholders are and their agendas
- Can build a cohesive team by being a motivator, coach, cheerleader, peacemaker, and conflict resolver
- Understands that the team will develop attitudes based on the emotions exhibited by this role, both positive and negative
- Always asks "what if" questions and avoids becoming comfortable with the current status of the project
- Manages time efficiently
- Above all, is able to plan, plan, plan

8. Select the Team Members

Your company is full of heroes. You know the people I mean...they're the ones who know how to get things done in your organization, even if they don't always work according to the organization's manual; those who have been consistently

With all their talent, they can't even build a simple four bedroom condo!

Bob The Beaver Builder

EAGER BEAVER CONSTRUCTION CREWS

more effective than their peers; those most eager to look for a better way to accomplish tasks; your long-term employees who often know as much about the business as the executive management team and, in some areas, maybe even more.

These heroes are your influencers, most capable of leading any transformation toward excellence, and these superstars must be the primary agents of change. If you can identify, train, and galvanize these key influencers, you will release tremendous organizational energy. The process must be quick—these types of employees have no tolerance for bureaucracy and wasted effort.

Look for heroes out in the field and as far away from headquarters as possible. Heroes generally spend most of their time with the customers. And be sure to seek out the most eager change leaders. Keep in mind that these workers may not be those who are formally recognized by the company, but rather are sought out by peers for answers. These are the employees who know which documented procedures don't work.

Be sure to have a good mixture of people from different areas and different levels within your organization.

Core team

The single biggest predictor of timely success is the team composition and level of dedication. The core team is responsible for performing the work that will ultimately achieve the objectives set forth in the mandate. The ideal team is composed of five to seven fully dedicated subject matter experts (in addition to the sponsor and the coach). All of the functions defined within the area under consideration should be represented within the team. The minimal amount of time that the team should dedicate to the effort is 51 percent of their total work hours. If there's less than a 51 percent time commitment, the team will have difficulty achieving results within the prescribed time.

A useful test when evaluating potential team members is to gauge the

---

DID YOU KNOW?

William Proctor, a candlemaker, and James Gamble, a soapmaker, were immigrants from England and Ireland respectively. They might not have met each other had they not married sisters, Olivia and Elizabeth Norris. Because both industries used similar resources, the panic of 1837 caused intense competition between the two, resulting in discord within the family. Their father-in-law called a meeting, at which he convinced his sons-in-law to become business partners. Proctor & Gamble was born in October 1837.[3]

reaction from their department managers when the candidate is proposed. Selecting high-performing people who are already well respected within the company sends a clear signal that management takes the program seriously. Moreover, a credible set of team members will be better able to drive change and implement recommendations.

Another important requirement for a successful program is active support from line management, which is why the team must be composed of frontline thought leaders. Time and again, change leaders discover that an "80 percent right" solution embraced and implemented by line managers beats the "100 percent right" solution that fails to win their acceptance. This buy-in rate is a critical indicator of success for this effort. It is essential for the team to socialize their ideas with line management and begin the implementation process early in the project.

Be careful: It is preferable that you not have managers and their direct reports on the team together, with the exception of the team leader. Having two people with a direct reporting relationship generally provides redundant insight to the team and may stifle the ability of the less senior member to contribute.

Ideal team members must:

- be well-respected thought leaders within the organization;
- "live" in the process on a daily basis and have a thorough understanding of how the process really works, not what is documented on the wall or in the system;
- be passionate about change and be open to new ideas;
- possess the ability to see the big picture;
- work well in a collaborative team environment and willingly commit to team goals;
- be able to make original contributions to team issues as well as build upon others' contributions;
- volunteer to execute commitment items and perform all assignments on time;
- positively question and challenge others as well as utilize conflicting views in a constructive manner;
- act to create and promote team cohesiveness;
- help maintain team spirit if things are going poorly;
- offer to relieve a team member's heavy workload;

- assume responsibility for problems;
- consider the impact on the external environment when developing potential solutions;
- selectively bring insights to the workplace as a crucial first step to effective implementation;
- understand that their responsibilities to the team are their primary professional responsibility;
- recognize that their role is not just another thing on an already full plate but rather an honor that will have a high impact on company performance;
- bring insights and analysis to the meetings and not simply supply data;
- be willing to ask tough questions and challenge conventional wisdom; and
- assist the team leader with meeting management, documentation, and discussions.

Organizations that overlook the importance of building a high-performing team of heroes risk failure. The following situation occurs at almost every new client meeting I have. I'm sitting at one of those long conference tables with about ten other people, including the CFO, a couple of people from marketing, two VPs from sales, and maybe the president. Together, we've chosen a couple of the company's most important strategic initiatives to consider as a starting place. I've just gone through a list of critical issues and have given them a solid justification for why we need six frontline people (out of a company of, say, ten thousand employees) for one calendar month. Sure, these are key people. But they're essential to this team.

Sometimes my initial justification isn't good enough, because invariably half the room presses me by saying, "Wow…six people for a month seems like an awfully long time. Can't you do it faster?" Then they say, "Maybe we should wait six months until the business cycle ends," or "We're operating awfully lean and don't have these extra resources just hanging out at the water cooler." Then they finally ask, "How do other companies do it?"

DID YOU KNOW?

Lou Holtz, legendary Notre Dame football coach, asks three questions when he builds a team: Do you care about me? Can I trust you? Are you committed to the success of this team?[4]

I tell them that other companies recognize how essential it is to the future of the company, we figure out the issue, and we move forward.

Satellite team

The satellite team serves a supporting role and has anywhere from one to ten members who act more as a collection of individuals than as a fully functioning team. These individuals can provide specific knowledge that is often not represented within the core team and might be peripheral to the team mandate. Their time commitment is generally no more than 5 percent.

At one energy company I worked with, for example, the core team used the satellite team, which was staffed with mid-level engineers, as a sounding board. The teams jointly tested and proposed ideas, won approval for standardization of procedures and controls, and acted as a channel to the greater organization. This approach proved to be highly effective because communication barriers were lowered and expanded teamwork created greater buy-in for the improvements.

For your satellite team, consider selecting members who represent IT, Finance, Legal, Human Resources, Compliance, managers from relevant areas, and very experienced personnel not currently serving on the core team. These people can offer you tremendous support.

Be careful: For both your core team and your satellite team, watch out for the following personality types:

- Knowledge suppressor
- Unwilling collaborator
- Pessimist
- Squelcher
- People diagnoser
- Dominator
- Flaw-finder
- Naysayer

They'll destroy an otherwise good team every time.

DID YOU KNOW?

When the following tactics are applied to transformation efforts, the success rate jumps from 30 percent to 80 percent:

- Setting clear and high aspirations and targets
- Exercising strong leadership from the top
- Creating an unambiguous structure for the transformation
- Maintaining energy and involvement throughout the organization[5]

9. Secure Dedicated Team Space and Team Requirements

The last step should be a relatively easy one (although, truth be told, I have had more than a few clients tell me this is the single most difficult step in the entire Q-Loop). Prior to the team kickoff, the sponsor should secure a dedicated meeting room to accommodate the entire team plus several guests. This will rapidly become known as the team's war room, where they will be papering the walls with process maps, graphs, charts, interview notes, and more. The team will likely require at least the following:

- A large supply of Post-it Notes (I prefer landscape 5" x 7" in different colors)
- Markers in different colors
- At least two flip chart stands
- Plenty of self-stick paper flip charts
- A coffee maker

You're Now Ready for the Next Step

Once you've accomplished these nine steps for getting started, you are ready to move on to the next step. It's a big one. And an exciting one. In fact, it's the game changer.

CHAPTER 4 TAKEAWAY

This phase of the Q-Loop—focusing on a mandate and forming a team of heroes—is perhaps the most critical of all.

Moving beyond "conference room solutions" and fully embracing your organization's IQ not only to ideate but to actualize change is what will allow you to successfully implement new initiatives.

Getting started doesn't require substantial capital investment. Instead, it requires that you identify a mandate and build the right team to achieve it.

If you carefully follow the nine steps of the getting-started process, you will be well positioned to achieve tremendous success.

COMING UP

In the next chapter, you'll discover how to see into the future—literally. Through the exercises and insights I'll offer you, you'll be able to foresee the outcome of your change initiative before you even embark on it. As a result, you will create an unprecedented groundswell of pull for your change initiative. Ready?

5

The Corporate Lab: The Art of the Possible

The real voyage of discovery consists not in seeking new landscapes, but in having new eyes.

—MARCEL PROUST

Anybody who has been seriously engaged in scientific work of any kind realizes that over the entrance to the gates of the temple of science are written the words: 'Ye must have faith.'

—MAX PLANCK

If this book has a beating heart, it is this chapter and the next. When I say this, I realize that I am merely using a metaphor, but it feels like so much more than that to me. Since beginning my journey of writing *The Q-Loop*, I knew that it would be these chapters that would deliver the blood and much of the life-sustaining nourishment to the rest of the book. If the other chapters are a map that leads you to great reward, chapters 5 and 6 are the key. If the rest of the book is a manned rocket ship, these are the rocket boosters.

The content for these chapters also derives from the very epicenter of my professional career since founding The Klapper Institute. From my early days, I recognized that most organizations aspire to deploy significant change programs, only to find them nearly impossible to implement. The reason is that successful change requires more than a vision and a coherent strategy. It also requires a workforce that not only doesn't resist change, but embraces it.

To achieve success, an organization must build a transformation program that will allow change to be rapidly pulled across its departments and throughout its layers. Unless key thought leaders at all levels—the heroes we discussed in chapter 4—embrace the change, the initiative will die on the vine. To create this kind of widespread passion, the workforce must be exposed to *what could be*, which will enable them to rethink their mental models, break free from their entrenched paradigms, and embrace the opportunity to learn.

This chapter will present a version of—as much as a book can replace the elaborate, real-world experience of the true thing—a fundamentally transformative, proprietary experience I named The Corporate Lab™. The Corporate Lab is a unique force that drives the ability to produce lasting change around the Q-Loop and one that I have personally witnessed redefine the mind-set and cultural attitudes within dozens of organizations. It is also the next step toward achieving a lasting change initiative after focusing on a compelling mandate and forming a team of heroes.

When I created The Corporate Lab, my goal was to establish a highly flexible, scalable, reality-based platform that would build clients' capabilities in a number of different areas. I wanted to deliver a transformative—not merely an educational—experience. Instead of morphing a textbook into an experience, I wanted to teach concepts that would show participants how to recognize obstacles to success in their own organization and how to overcome them. To achieve these lofty objectives, I knew I needed to immerse participants in an environment that would precisely mirror their day-to-day workplace in terms of culture and behavior, so that they could truly see how they typically behave. The basic philosophy of the Lab is that it weaves together traditional problem solving, in the form of the scientific method, and a strong constructivist element.

The scientific method challenges you to make an observation, ask a question, form a hypothesis, conduct an experiment, and then accept or reject your hypothesis. This is the backbone of the problem-solving approach we use in the Lab. However, the scientific method isn't enough to generate the behavioral change that's crucial to allowing participants to experience the "art of the possible." The Lab therefore employs a heavy dose of constructivism.

Constructivism is a learning theory defined by Seymour Papert of the MIT Media Lab. It holds that students learn best when making sense of something on their own with the teacher as a guide to help them along the way. Along these lines, the Lab lets participants discover (see how they are performing today), dream (understand what their company is capable of), desire (want to make the changes to realize future state), and reach their destiny (embody the confidence the Lab engenders to believe that change is not merely possible but certain).

As a result, the Lab was constructed to absorb the cultural norms of the client organization. This familiarity encourages participants to reframe their mindsets by allowing them to view the same information that they have seen countless times through a very different lens. This new way of viewing their organization and themselves enables them to recalibrate their perspective and become open to change.

Since The Corporate Lab experience is neither preprogrammed nor scripted, and pressure is high and timing is short, all critical interactions and intuitive decisions emerge organically from the participants. These actions are identical to the responses the participants make in their workplace. Senior managers in the Lab are bombarded with potential decisions and the way they prioritize their time dramatically shapes the experience for everyone, driving financial, operating, individual, and cultural performance.

The Corporate Lab's ability to condense time and space is the most effective way I have witnessed to uncover employees' intuitive response to stimuli and to show them how their behavior contributes to or detracts from organizational value. Time and again, my beliefs have been confirmed by participants.

The Lab works by allowing participants to learn and implement the Q-Loop in just two days. Participants become employees at a company rife with familiar problems, issues, and challenges. Participants try to improve this company using the same approaches they use in their own organization, with minimal success. Participants are then introduced to the Q-Loop and shown how to solve entrenched problems with an entirely fresh perspective and approach.

Getting you from where you are today to where you want to be in the future, The Corporate Lab helps you prepare your culture to embrace any major change initiative by reframing your approach. It can be used to prepare you for anything from strategy development to growth, from redefining your organizational structure to preparing for an IT implementation or achieving operational excellence.

Birth of The Corporate Lab

From the time I was in business school until the *aha!* moment when I knew that I must form a company that would be fundamentally different from any other management consulting business, I wrestled with how to deliver lasting change to organizations. I had successes, certainly, but too often I noted that many of these successes faded with time. I knew there must be a better way to make change last, and to be able to teach organizations to repeat the process ad infinitum, even after The Klapper Institute was no longer actively assisting the organization with a specific change initiative. My goal, always, is to teach clients how to autonomously deliver future improvement projects.

Then one day in 2005, I had an epiphany. I was on a Metro-North train, heading from my home in Connecticut toward the center of Manhattan, gliding through the deep recesses of the dark final approach to Grand Central Terminal, when suddenly a scene from a movie popped into my head. It was *The Untouchables*.

In the movie, Eliot Ness, played by Kevin Costner, needs to assemble a team of officers to pursue Al Capone, played unforgettably by Robert DeNiro. But finding cops who Ness could trust and who weren't corrupt was proving next to impossible. You see, one of the reasons Capone had become "untouchable" was that just about every cop in Chicago was on his payroll. Sean Connery, playing a wise old Irish cop named Jim Malone, suggests that Costner should change his tactic and get rookie cops right out of the police academy. Connery growled to Costner, "If you're afraid of getting a rotten apple, don't go to the barrel. Get it off the tree."

For days, I couldn't get the quote out of my thoughts.

When it came time for me to build the transformative experience that I knew was necessary to help companies see themselves differently, the experience that would allow them to live into the future of their change initiative and learn to see their stumbling blocks as well as the path to success, the obvious choice would have been for me to go to an engineering firm or a workshop development agency or a training organization. But that would be like going to the barrel for the apple. I didn't want people in their forties or fifties repackaging their tired ideas with the new veneer of my specifications.

Instead, I decided to pluck the juiciest apples right from the healthiest tree in the lushest orchard to create the freshest, most profound experience.

The MIT Media Lab is arguably the most fertile ground for the smartest thinkers about technology in the nation, if not the world. I hired from the MIT Media Lab five of the brightest minds I've ever had the pleasure to work with, and I told them at the outset of the project that I wanted something that no one had ever seen or experienced before. I stipulated, "I want you to custom create a new set of technologies to construct a unique experience that even the most jaded participant will go through and say, 'Wow, that was incredible!'"

> **DID YOU KNOW?**
>
> The One Laptop Per Child program grew out of a research effort conducted at the MIT Media Lab. The program led to the creation of affordable, portable educational devices to be used in the developing world.[1]

We developed an experience that is fluid and natural-feeling on the surface but is incredibly complex under the hood. Because it is not a canned experience, because it is not scripted, and because participants dictate what will happen, the experience of The Corporate Lab can never be the same twice. The number of variables is limitless. Over the two-day experience of The Corporate Lab, the culture of the organization emerges, with all its frustrations, defects, quirks, and strengths. In other words, The Corporate Lab mirrors the culture of the participating organization, yet it compresses time to enable expansive learning to happen in a small window of time.

The Corporate Lab Is Not a "Simulation"

When the uninitiated hear about The Corporate Lab and assume that it's a simulation, I bristle. A simulation it is not—at least not in any way that people commonly think of the term.

Other firms have indeed created business simulators in an attempt to help organizations accelerate the pace of achieving initiatives. In some cases, they claim to have created accurate representations of reality. Yet, in the firms' descriptions of these simulations, they repeatedly use the descriptor "game" or "gamelike environment" to describe the simulation.

I have studied these simulations/games and they, in fact, feel very much like the adventure games my son sometimes plays on his (highly regulated) Xbox or like the board game Monopoly that my family plays together on our game nights. As such, the experience of these business simulations feels radically different from the day-to-day realities of any organization I have ever worked with. And I doubt very much that they accurately capture the complexity of your organization. True simulators, on the other hand—the kinds used for operating room procedures or for training nuclear power plant operators—are so fundamentally realistic down to the most minute detail that you can't tell the difference between them and the real thing.

In the end, most simulator-based training efforts fail because they don't reproduce the organization's intricacies, which prevents employees from easily applying the learning in on-the-job situations. And it is this immediate transfer of learning to real-world applications that can generate the rapid results necessary to sustain the initiative. Unless the experience allows participants to declare *this is us!*, the ability to drive behavioral change is minimal.

DID YOU KNOW?

The nuclear simulator Sequoia is a supercomputer built by IBM. Rated the most powerful computer in the world, it has 1.5 million processing cores and can do 16.3 quadrillion calculations per second—more than any machine ever built. Among other scientific purposes, Sequoia simulates nuclear explosions without the need to test actual nuclear bombs.[2]

Like a car-driving video game, in which a player can weave in and out of traffic, drive eighty miles per hour through a school zone, and not worry about knocking over pedestrians— because nothing is really at stake—a business simulation has nothing at stake. So workers become players and the business becomes a game.

The Corporate Lab, on the other hand, is not a simulation in this sense. It is not a game. Instead, it is a very real business experience during which participants become immersed in a painstakingly detailed environment that is nearly identical to their day-to-day workplace and that enables them to see how they typically behave under a range of conditions. In the hundreds of Labs that I've conducted, I've seen tears, cheers, frustration, joy, and every other emotion on the spectrum. That's because the Lab captures reality so fully and meticulously. As a result, and because of the way that The Corporate Lab unfolds over its two days, participants recognize how to shift their behavior to consistently succeed in an ongoing fashion.

While I wish that I could work with readers of this book personally for two days and run the full Lab at their organizations, with their people, it's of course not possible to do so. But what I can do is share the experience of my many clients to offer you the opportunity to witness their transformation. As you witness them pass through the two days and multiple stages of the Lab, and read the choices they made and realizations they extracted from the experience, you will have the opportunity to apply useful aspects of the experience to yourself and to your own organization.

In addition to sharing the experience of The Corporate Lab, I will also include useful exercises and insights from my many years of running the Lab. Throughout this chapter, I encourage you to involve the members of your team of heroes, selected in chapter 4, in the exercises and experiences I share. It is through this process that your team will coalesce into a powerhouse of change.

Additional Skills to Support a Change Initiative

Keep in mind that, while the mind-set shift offered by The Corporate Lab is a powerful game changer, linking the way you work with this mind-set change is a vitally important component. Even The Corporate Lab can be undermined if you and your colleagues return to the same old operating environment afterward. That's why this chapter connects to the previous chapter and, even more importantly, to the next chapter, where we will discuss how to achieve an audacious change initiative. In the next chapter, you will also learn a number of hard skills, including how to conduct surveys, use analytics, apply process mapping, and more.

Normally taught as part of The Corporate Lab, these hard skills will prove indispensable to you. For the sake of clarity, I will focus primarily on the mind-set shift that occurs during The Corporate Lab in this chapter and then present the more analytic, strategic skills in chapter 6.

Another important consideration to keep in mind is that, while it is not possible for every reader to directly experience The Corporate Lab, it is imperative that your team experiences some sort of compelling mind-set-shifting experience before we move onto the next stage of the Q-Loop (in which we will take the mandate and the team of heroes and pursue the change initiative). Biased though I might be, The Corporate Lab is unrivaled in allowing organizations to break their current paradigm and discover new ways of working, and this chapter will reproduce enough of the Lab experience, along with additional exercises, to point you in the right direction. Still, it is up to you to take the time and ensure adequate commitment to the undertaking to generate a true mind-set shift.

Overview of The Corporate Lab

Before I offer a detailed accounting of The Corporate Lab and share the experience from a characteristic client's point of view, allow me to offer a brief overview of the Lab so that you grasp the basic trajectory of these two transformative days. That way, you'll better understand the context when I go into more detail in the remainder of the chapter.

Getting Started

Approximately twenty client participants assume job responsibilities of a new operating division of NAVCorp, which is a $270 million designer, manufacturer, and marketer of computer navigation–related products. The company includes everything from high-tech products and a process to manufacture them, to e-mail systems, product brochures, IT support, a call center, marketing plans, budgets, and an annual report. There's even a supply chain, with outside vendors and distributors. In a strict sense, NAVCorp is fictional, but I promise you that clients find it unquestionably real. Typically, participants take on very different roles from their current positions so that they gain new perspectives.

NAVCorp also has an organization chart that includes Human Resources, Finance, Sales, Customer Service, Distribution, Marketing, and Operations. Supplied with an electronic tablet for the two days, each participant can capture and manipulate data as well as exchange communications among the different roles. As I mentioned earlier, the experience is not a gamelike simulation, and this company exhibits the complexity and depth of the participants' organization.

Setting the Scene

The Corporate Lab takes place in approximately 1,600 feet of contiguous space with 20 participants from different parts of the client company. Each participant has an individual work space—front-line workers have cubicles and senior management has a conference room.

At kick-off, participants receive an important welcome kit: a letter from the CEO welcoming them to the team; an employee ID badge; an annual report; product and service brochures; and an HR package that includes roles and responsibilities, reporting relationships, and performance objectives. Next, a video from the CEO welcomes participants to the organization and a company overview video is watched by everyone.

Participants then receive their tablets, which are individually loaded with job requirements and calculator functions specific to each job. These tablets let participants send and receive emails and notifications, and perform the analysis required by the job. Results from the tablets are transmitted to a classroom for analysis, discussion, and debrief. As mentioned earlier, there is no script, and participants are guided by their specific objectives, their department's objectives, company objectives, their wisdom and experience, and good business judgment. These factors allow the culture of their organization to be imported into the Lab, which plays a very significant role in guiding the decisions that the participants make.

After roles, responsibilities, job descriptions, and other preliminary data and documents are distributed, we kick off fiscal year 1 (FY1) of NAVCorp.

FY1

During FY1, which occurs during the morning of day one, participants encounter a series of significant business challenges that can potentially cause customer defection. As a result, participants experience familiar stress, anxiety, time pressure, and inconsistent data, which leads to fatigue, frustration, and failure. They also directly experience how their conventional approaches to problem solving—firefighting, relying on tribal wisdom, and conference room solutions—are not sustainable. By the end of FY1, participants declare, "This is just like our organization!"

Later, during a debriefing session and an afternoon learning session, we conduct a financial, operational, individual, and cultural assessment. We then introduce and utilize The Klapper Institute's scientific method, called the Results Triangle, which includes the three Ls of Listen, Learn, and Launch, to make changes to the organization. As I mentioned, I'll go into more detail about these hard skills in the next chapter, so we can focus here on changing the mind-set of everyone involved. As clients learn the Results Triangle methodology, we begin to discuss how these new skills can be applied to NAVCorp (and, by implication, to their own organization).

NAVCorp Characteristics During FY1

- Not quick or agile; everything from decision making to execution takes far longer than it should
- Lacking awareness and alignment of enterprise-wide business operations
- Has a strong legacy-based structure dominated by entrenched silos
- Structurally inefficient, leading to redundancy, rework, high cost position, and delays
- Holds a widespread belief that customer-focus is important, but departmental goals and individual objectives are not aligned to achieve desired outcomes
- Lacking distributed leadership, so most key decisions are made hierarchically
- Focused on individual tasks rather than on processes that serve customers, leading to lack of repeatability, consistency, and predictability, with the work done differently each time it is performed

FY2

Fiscal Year 2 begins on the morning of the second day. FY2 helps participants experience how optimizing department-level performance without building connections across the organization fails to deliver the desired result. Participants start to feel the impact of internal focus versus customer focus and realize how bureaucracy inhibits a quick response to changing market conditions. In addition, they discover how hierarchical decision-making contributes to slowed actions.

During a FY2 debriefing, the strong connection between the lessons of NAVCorp and their own organization becomes even clearer. Client participants now make additional changes to NAVCorp based on all that they have learned and experienced.

NAVCorp Characteristics During FY2

- Stable but suboptimal organization, with well-entrenched silos and conflicting goals and measures
- Management begins to understand how it currently solves problems and realizes that the current approach is not as productive as it could be

- Employees realize that the purpose of their work is to deliver exceptional value, not to satisfy departmental goals
- Employees begin to set stretch performance targets that begin to align to company and customer objectives

FY3

During the second and final afternoon of the Lab, participants operate FY3 of NAVCorp and apply all of the knowledge, new skills, and—most important—radically new perspective to make dramatic performance gains across all financial, operational, and cultural measures. Employees now also recognize that change is inevitable and they embrace it as an ongoing part of their professional life.

NAVCorp Characteristics During FY3

- Clear understanding of and aggressive pursuit of company strategy
- Intense performance-driven environment tempered by what participants say is "an outstanding place to work"
- Dramatic performance gains across all financial, operational, individual, and cultural measures
- Recognition among employees that change is inevitable and they embrace it
- Simple, clearly understood organizational structure accompanied by lean, efficient processes
- Clear accountability throughout the organization
- Effective, timely communication across all silos and levels
- An overriding wish "never to return to NAVCorp FY1"

Kicking Off The Corporate Lab

Let me share with you the way I often begin The Corporate Lab. One of the key questions I ask is, "When confronted with change, what is your intuitive response to it?" It's imperative that you understand how you instinctively respond to change, so that you can evaluate and determine whether your response leads you to the best course of action. To help you ascertain the answer, consider the following scenario, which I present to every client participant at the beginning of each Corporate Lab.

You're driving down a narrow, two-lane road. It's a beautiful day. You're singing along with the song on the stereo. Houses with front lawns are on both sides of the road. You're a safe driver so you're doing the speed limit of thirty-five miles per hour. Out of nowhere, a six-year-old child runs after a bouncing ball right in front of your car.

What do you do?

It's likely you slam on your brakes.

Where are you looking?

Likely at the child.

What are you thinking?

I hope I stop in time.

Now compare this to racecar driving school, which I was rash enough to once attend. As I drove a Mazda MX-5 around the track, coached to accelerate more and more by my instructor, who sat in the passenger seat— 120 mph... 130 mph—I was told to avoid the pylons set out on the track. I was feeling confident as I streaked past one pylon, then another, then suddenly someone threw a pylon onto the track in front of me. It bounced. I jammed the brake pedal down as hard as I could. *Smack!* The pylon hit the windshield.

My copilot told me to once again speed up. Again, *blam!* Another pylon tossed onto the track, another failed attempt to stop the racecar in time. Again and again, pylon after pylon was thrown in front of me and, again and again, I failed to stop in time. The instructor told me to pull in for a pit stop.

He turned to my red face and said, "Brian, the object is to *avoid* slamming into the pylons, not to hit them."

"I get it," I said sheepishly. "I guess I'm just not very good at this."

He laughed. "Well, if it makes you feel any better, no one can bring a two-ton car down from 140 to zero in that amount of space. It's impossible. This time, let's try something different."

Sounded good to me.

"The moment you get the first glimpse of that orange pylon, instead of hitting the brakes, hit the accelerator. And instead of looking at the pylon, why don't you look in the direction that you'd like the car to go, then go there?" he suggested

It went against every instinct. It seemed just plain wrong and even reckless. But I nodded.

I pulled back onto the track, picked up speed, and kept my eyes peeled for a glimpse of orange being thrown in my path. When a pylon appeared out of nowhere, I responded differently. This time I avoided it by looking left, veering that direction, and accelerating sharply. Pylon after pylon I avoided. Going against every initial impulse, I relearned how to see the event and, as a result, I changed the outcome—not just once but each and every time.

Now, the moral of the story isn't necessarily to put the pedal to the metal the next time a kid jumps in front of your car. The point is that we need to learn to see things differently, which is the fundamental benefit of The Corporate Lab.

Experiencing The Corporate Lab

Let's look at a representative client composite to experience a semblance of The Corporate Lab. As you read the account of this organization experiencing the Lab, think about your own organization and consider whether you are similar and, if yes, how so. From my experience, many of the same attributes rear their head at an overwhelming majority of the organizations I work with, which is why I created a composite organization for this section. My hope is that you will see enough of your own organization in it to indirectly experience what an organization goes through when participating in The Corporate Lab.

Coming into the Lab

Senior management says...	Client associates say...
"Nothing else has worked so let's give this program a try."	"So this is the new flavor of the month."
"Our senior management team can't agree on how to proceed."	"Has our management team gone through this?"
"Although I have a clear sense of what we need to do (and how to act), my colleagues just don't get it."	"I hate this kind of stuff!"
"I know what needs to be done, but I don't have the right people or resources to do it."	"Since management already knows what they want to do, I don't get why we need to go through this exercise."
"If we only had better technology, our problem would be solved."	"I really don't have the time for this right now."
"Transformation is a discrete program with a well-defined beginning, middle, and end."	"This has absolutely nothing to do with doing my job...or with me."

The leadership style of this organization coming into The Corporate Lab is command and control, so the organization tends to be run in a top-down fashion. The organization is risk averse, with a high fear of failure, and so avoids instability at almost any cost. A phrase team members use to describe their own organization is "belt and suspenders," which makes me chuckle. It's a vivid way to describe a no-risk culture that always has a backup plan in case the first way fails. While thoroughness can be an asset, such avoidance of failure stands in direct opposition to the healthy organizational culture I described in chapter 1.

Next, the organization has a notable lack of awareness and alignment around enterprise-wide processes. What that means is that there's a strong legacy-based work structure that is firmly entrenched and dominated by concrete silos. Ideas, changes, and developments can move within a silo fairly efficiently, but moving from silo to silo is extremely difficult and happens at a glacial pace.

While the organization believes that customer focus matters, many of the department goals and individual objectives don't connect to what the outcomes are for the customer. Instead, there's a strong focus on individual tasks rather than on end-to-end processes because of entrenched work structures. The consequence is that there is a lack of repeatability, consistency, and predictability, so work is done differently almost every time it's performed.

The tendency among most participants in this client organization is toward complying with organizational rules, policies, regulations, and standards rather than on real commitment to do the job well and serve customers in the best way they can. It's not a surprise. In a command-and-control, risk-averse environment, policies dominate and so employees aren't able to use common sense and sound judgment to make decisions and to get truly passionate about the work being done. Another outcome of such an environment is that employees are dependent instead of empowered, and blame tends to be assigned instead of employees taking full accountability for their own or their team's actions.

I bring up to the team the subject of pursuing controlled failure—a phrase that has admittedly been used almost to death in recent years, yet there is still value in the concept of being bold enough to risk coming up short on an endeavor. The twenty people in the room—particularly the members of senior management—look at each other as if to say, "Why would we ever want to fail at anything?" I share a story about Bank of

America, which expects a 30 percent failure rate of the experiments it runs. I don't think they're buying the value of such a "foolhardy" attitude. It's okay with me. I like the challenge.

A final characteristic of the organization is that it takes a short-term reactive approach over a long-term proactive approach. Because the organization is running lean, it's all these people can do to manage their day jobs. They believe intellectually that having a long-term view and being proactive is a smart approach, but they are focused on the relentless barrage of day-to-day activities. I suspect some members are skeptical—and even a little irked—that they're being dragged away from their other duties to participate in the Lab. Still, management wants to change this cultural profile; otherwise they wouldn't have asked me to come into their organization.

What I know is that the Lab is about to spark something that can seem almost magical. The participants sitting with me in this large training space don't yet realize it. It's an exhilarating moment for me.

Do any of the descriptions of this organization sound familiar? My suspicion is that at least some of them do. Let's now witness this organization going through The Corporate Lab. I believe you'll see a good bit of yourself in the decisions, insights, and experiences.

Morning of Day One—Learning to See Yourself

Senior management says...	Client associates say...
"Working in NAVCorp fiscal year 1 was one of the toughest things I have ever had to do."	"As NAVCorp's director of operations, it was incredibly frustrating trying to lead without having anyone follow. I now know how management feels."
"Working as an assembler in the Lab, I now realize how disempowered our frontline associates must feel."	"I really enjoyed the discussion on rework. That's all my department really does."
"I never realized how much of my workday I spend in unproductive meetings."	"The facilitators kept stressing 'focused and disciplined thinking.' Our group really struggled with that."
"I always thought that a complicated problem needed a complex and expensive solution."	"I am exhausted...I've never had to think so much in my life!"

(continued)

Senior management says...	Client associates say...
"It's amazing how simple an answer can be if you really understand the problem."	"It's amazing that under tight dead-lines, data and analysis go out the window and we all reverted to gut feel."
"The discussion around the problem-solving matrix was very interesting—we need more fact-based decision making around here."	"I cannot believe that 80 percent of what I do every day adds absolutely no value to the organization."
"It's shocking to see that under stress I tend to make the same kinds of decisions over and over again—and they're not always the right ones."	"Wow, the opportunity for improvement in one company is enormous."

We assign the roles for fiscal year 1 at NAVCorp. We decide to put more senior people on the front line in production so they remember what it's like, and we put some of the high-potential frontline workers in managerial roles so they can get a taste of decision making. Nobody wants to be the division president. The cultural dynamic of the organization is now positioned to unfold before us.

Over in the production area of NAVCorp, which is set up along the back wall of our space, production is doing some complicated electronics assembly of navigational gyroscopes, which the company sells to its demanding clients. All goes well... for a while.

The boss leaves the sheltered bubble of his office and passes through production. Soon, he notices a backup. He hovers over a production worker (in this case, a senior manager is on production and a frontline worker is the boss), and demands to know why.

The assembly worker says she is working as fast as she can but that she's not getting the materials she needs. It's meaningful to note here that there are a number of rules set up at NAVCorp. For example, there is a rule that states that production must use up all existing materials before they can order new materials. The result is that production sometimes is forced to sit idle while they wait for new materials to be delivered. Other clients would have ignored this rule from minute one (which would have created other problems), but this client follows the rule, not even questioning where the rule came from, how old it is, or why it exists.

The boss, trying to speed up production, makes an intuitive decision.

At a significant percentage of past Corporate Labs I've run, the worker has gotten fired; this boss doesn't do that, but it's a close call as the boss asks the worker to switch jobs with someone in a different department who seems to be working faster. It's most definitely not a fact-based decision.

Assembly continues to run behind in production and, no surprise, NAVCorp customers are getting frustrated. The assembly department looks to purchase an external solution to speed up production and so they inquire about a piece of technology that will allow them to assemble faster. Another conference room solution, I think, and note that we should discuss it in the afternoon, after FY1. Assembly invests $5 million in the automated solution. It does speed up assembly within that particular silo of the organization. Was that the core issue, however? Was slow assembly the actual system constraint? Was this money well spent?

As production pushes along and the customer deadline draws near, I notice all the managers gathering around a quality assurance (QA) person, who sits there in the last stage of production of a critical circuit board, his safety goggles in place. A total of seven managers look over his shoulder, "helping" him do his job. They're worried about not shipping on time. I'm tempted to make a joke about this organization's interesting take on "overhead" as they literally hang over his head, but I just observe the happenings. The QA person doesn't need their help, having worked flawlessly on dozens of circuit boards all morning. But with them breathing down his neck, he's nervous, and he makes a mistake. The circuit board now has to be reworked and they miss a deadline. I wonder how often this sort of scenario occurs in their actual organization.

Happening simultaneously within NAVCorp, the customer service call center (again, staffed by a range of client participants) is getting slammed with calls and e-mails from NAVCorp customers, who are beginning to get frustrated by delivery delays and quality-control issues, among other concerns. The IT system is functional but not great, and customer service reps are doing their best to manage the load. In fact, I'm impressed by how heroically the reps are trying to handle the deluge.

Meanwhile, the HR director is evaluating customer service performance using standard objective metrics (how many calls were received, how many were handled satisfactorily, and so on) and determining that the call center is achieving only about 40 percent of their objective. As a result, the organization is receiving customer complaints. HR, therefore, hammers the call center. Finally, the primary rep of the customer service call center gets fired and someone else is put into the position. Emotions are running a bit high and the person replaced is visibly shaken. She was, after all, working valiantly to achieve the organization's objective.

The customer call center has some automated solutions to increase their success rate. Other solutions, however, are outside of the scope of what their system can handle, so they scramble to figure out other fixes by talking to other employees and groups at NAVCorp who can potentially help them. For now, FY1 progresses, but I note that this scenario will be essential to address during the upcoming debrief.

Other events transpire during day one—NAVCorp's stock price drops and its revenue declines—but I hope you can clearly see how the organization's established culture emerged from the client as they assumed the helm of NAVCorp. As the day unfolded, it felt far from a simulation of a company. It became a real company with a real culture and real problems. When this team of top-notch people fell shy of their lofty expectations for themselves, they were stunned and unhappy. It's an interesting dynamic to witness, and to experience.

Afternoon of Day One—Learning to Understand Yourself

During the debriefing and learning session that occurs immediately following NAVCorp day one, we analyze NAVCorp's stock performance, which was driven by the participants' decisions. We analyze the company's revenue, its labor and materials costs, its profit margin, and numerous other detailed NAVCorp FY1 measures and results.

We then address the rule that prevented the assembly worker from working at peak performance, which represents so many rules and processes deeply entrenched at organizations, including the client's own. I ask, "Why did you guys go ahead and wait for all material to appear before working on the next piece of work?"

The response is: "Well, that's the rule."

I say, "Do you understand the genesis of that rule?"

"No," they answer.

"Were you curious about the genesis of the rule?"

"No," they say, showing no apparent sign of defensiveness about the answer. "It's a rule."

Part of me respects the answer. After all, rules are meant to be followed. Yet, I wonder why they don't question the origin of the rule and the value of it. In the case of NAVCorp, this material-transfer rule had been put in place about four decades earlier by corporate audit because the company was receiving too much material, so controls were put into place. The control was that all material needed to be used before more material could be purchased. The rule is outdated. Yet no one questioned it until prompted to do so. It's understandable that participants have this point of view, even if, from the outside looking in, it seems that they should have thought to question the current way of doing things.

But think about it like this: if you've ever sold your house, you were probably surprised and shocked by the objective evaluations offered by the broker or real estate agent, who rather cold-heartedly told you all the things you should change before selling your beloved home. You were the one, after all, to paint the living room that color and pick out that chandelier and those rugs. It's the same thing in organizations, where people tend not to think about how things are done because they don't have the time or the motivation, or they have just overlooked them. Additionally, if an individual—particularly on the front line—notices a better way of getting things done, there is often resistance somewhere up the chain of command or there is no effective way to share ideas, as discussed in part 1 of the book.

Next during the debrief, we discuss the shortcomings of the call center. Rather quickly we discern that, regardless of who was in the position of customer service representative, he would have had an impossible time keeping up with the workload. What I know from the many Labs I've run is that the person today was actually better than most. But this kind of organization, which is all about the numbers and which has a conservative outlook, tends to blame the person in the role and not the process leading to the failure.

I ask, "How often does this sort of thing occur at your organization?"

The answer is that a number of positions at the client's actual organization have a revolving door.

"So maybe it's not about the people you bring in," I say. My experience at most organizations—in both the public and the private sector—is that 95 percent of the people are quite capable and motivated. "Maybe you have a system where it's impossible for some roles to be successful."

Interestingly, the call center rep was fired without her manager having any real understanding of why she wasn't able to keep up with the call load. Yet she was fired nonetheless. The HR director decided that something needed to change and so the person in the role was replaced. It's a conference room solution if ever I've seen one. A fact-based analysis would have revealed why the customer was unhappy, what the customer service rep was doing day to day, what the call center system was able to handle, what their process was, and what the constraints placed on the customer service rep were.

Furthermore, a simple analysis might have revealed that the customer service rep was handling a hundred calls per hour—a Herculean accomplishment—while the call center was receiving two hundred calls per hour. So an employee who should have been heralded as a hero was instead fired.

It's a powerful moment when everyone realizes the paradox of the situation, and it offers a real learning experience. We'll discuss these analytical tools, which will help you to develop more fact-based solutions, in the next chapter.

Regarding the assembly-line backup and the decision of the boss to switch workers reactively, what the boss failed to see was that the assembly worker didn't get his shipment of new boards until five minutes earlier and then started to work fast. The boss only saw the backup of boards and didn't determine the root cause.

And when motor assembly subsequently fell behind the production schedule, the assessment was that they could speed up the process by purchasing new technology tools. What management never fully understood, however—because they didn't do a fact-based analysis—was that some of the arbitrary work rules were responsible for the slowdown. It's not at all that the motor assembly was falling behind. Contrary to what management believed, motor assembly was ahead of spec. (They were required to do a motor assembly every five minutes and they were doing it every three-and-a-half or four minutes.)

Both solutions were the result of the command-and-control culture of this organization as they ran NAVCorp.

Now, please don't be misled into believing that any organization that goes through The Corporate Lab is set up for predetermined failure. NAVCorp is not set up to drive the participating organization toward imminent failure. I will say, however, that many organizations have experienced the Lab, and they have all, in one way or another, gotten in their own way because of aspects of their embedded culture that emerge during the two-day event. For example, when the pressure was on during FY1, some of the employees stepped into different roles to help out. This shows a collaborative team at work, but it was yet another conference room solution. They tried to help each other out but not everyone was able to work at a level that actually helped, and sometimes they even created more problems.

For the remainder of the day, we dive deep into The Klapper Institute's scientific method for problem solving, called the Results Triangle, to address some of NAVCorp's difficulties (and, by implication, their own organization's). We'll cover the Results Triangle in the next chapter, where you will learn to address many of your organization's most challenging issues as you prepare to implement the mandate you identified in chapter 4.

The group uncovers that many of the individual participants performed admirably within their particular silo, meeting their distinct objectives, but these individual accomplishments didn't necessarily link up to the overall organizational objectives, which really are tied to customer objectives. That disconnect was what led to the company's downturn.

I turn to a member of senior management and ask, "Does that resonate with how your actual organization operates?"

With no hesitation, he says, "Absolutely."

Around the table, heads nod.

He adds, "I'm constantly getting pounded by the board because overall performance is down. Meanwhile, my frontline workers are asking for their bonuses because they're meeting individual objectives."

We begin to discuss how to improve the overall organizational performance within NAVCorp. One of the main discussions we have, and which sparks some heated conversation around the table, is who the company's customers are. I know I've touched a nerve and that the debate—although on the surface it's about NAVCorp—is really getting to an essential debate within the client's own organization. I take a strong position that there is no such thing as an "internal customer." It's one of my least favorite phrases in the English language. But my assertion runs counter to the beliefs of some of the participants.

I think about the many insurance company clients I've run the Lab for. During those Labs, the insurance company participants invariably ask, "Aren't agents our customers?" I'm aware that they treat them as customers, wining and dining them, taking them to lavish offsite events. They go on to say, "Without these agents, we're out of business." Now, I in no way would ever suggest to an insurance company that they shouldn't treat their agents like gold, but I do say—in no uncertain terms—that their agents ARE NOT their customers.

To this group, I say, "At the end of the day, there's only one customer group. And those are the people who pay the bill. If they walk away, you have no business. The day you lose sight of who your customer really is, that's the day you put your business in tremendous peril."

In addition to the insurance industry, I cite the familiar example of the American auto industry losing sight of who its customers were in the 1970s. At that time, Detroit started to build cars based on what auto dealers wanted to sell, but, of course, the dealers had their own profit margin and self-interest at heart. Meanwhile, actual car buyers—the real customers—turned to smaller, fuel-efficient foreign cars. Participants' heads start to move up and down as they see my point.

We then spend the remainder of the afternoon diving deep into the Results Triangle, including learning how to survey the customer. We perform a number of analytic techniques to determine where the organization is today in terms of strategy and operations (we use NAVCorp in our examples, but the methods translate to the participating organization). We develop hypotheses for new strategies to pursue new operational and organizational improvements. Much of this approach is shockingly new to the participants. We design and run experiments to prove or disprove all of the hypotheses—which tends to be a challenge, because most groups want to jump over this step and get right to solutions.

RESISTANT INDUSTRIES OPERATING PRINCIPLE #29
"Don't worry about why we do things the way we do.
Leave that to management."

I tell them, "Solutions are worth pennies; root causes are worth millions." It's counterintuitive to these smart, results-oriented people. We then build pilots to demonstrate our new capabilities and thoroughly test them before implementation.

At the risk of frustrating you, dear reader, for I suspect you are also a very smart, results-oriented person, I ask you to consider this description of the afternoon of day one to be a tease for the next chapter, where I will explain these capabilities. Please keep in mind that this chapter focuses primarily on learning to see who you are now, so that you are more effectively positioned to implement the mandate you've selected. We'll learn the tools outlined here soon enough.

IDEAS IN ACTION

The fastest-growing city in Canada, Barrie, is located on Lake Simcoe in northeastern Ontario. The city sought not only to improve the overall efficiency and effectiveness of the municipality's services, but also to transform the culture of an organization in which the average employee tenure was nearly twenty years.

Barrie had spent three years working with many external experts to help with its transformation—without any real success. In each case, the story was essentially the same: the strong organizational culture deeply rooted in preserving the status quo repeatedly resisted and ultimately defeated all management-led change efforts. As employees of the municipality, workers enjoyed essentially lifetime employment and, as a result, never felt particularly compelled to embrace change.

In a conversation we had for this book, Ed Archer, general manager of corporate services and the project sponsor for the Klapper project, reflected on how projects traditionally ran at the city of Barrie. He said, "Historically, a staff team would have been put together made up of people whom the senior team thought were the right group to put that project in play. It would have been one of the things on their to-do list. There would have been issues with scheduling meetings and coordinating work among departments. They would have had the same competing priorities that have always plagued a conglomerate like a government organization."

Working with The Klapper Institute, the city finally took a different approach. It put the executive leadership team and the fifteen heroes who were historically viewed as the leaders of the resistance through The Corporate Lab. By the end of the event, they had completely

(continued)

transformed NAVCorp, had optimized organizational performance, and, most importantly, had become excited about tackling these targeted issues in their municipality. The Lab got them to *think* differently. It prepared them for the next big step.

It's interesting to note that, prior to working with The Klapper Institute, many city leaders were concerned that employee motivation and the sense of entrepreneurship would be too fundamentally different among city employees, compared with a corporation's, for the project to be a success. Kathleen Short, manager of revenue for the city of Barrie and a project team member, informed me during an interview for the book, "The Klapper project was fully supported by upper management, although council was a bit skeptical. A few of us on the team had tried for several years to address this issue and were close to giving up. We felt this had become a do or die situation."

Evidently, a strong enough case was made to proceed with the project. But I'll never forget being asked by the project sponsor during our first Corporate Lab debrief what the difference was between this team and my "normal" Corporate Lab experiences with large corporations. I told him, "Absolutely nothing." And it was true.

Immediately following the Lab, Barrie created two teams and gave each a thirty-day time limit, full support, and access to the tools they needed to achieve difficult change mandates. Within twenty-one days, both teams had coupled customer insights with their deep and latent knowledge of how to really get things done—and translated them into experiments and pilots that far exceeded their mandates. In fact, one of the teams developed a working pilot that will save the city millions of dollars for many years to come. Both projects have since been fully implemented, and the level of passion for the change was unprecedented.

Ed Archer went on to point out some of the differences between earlier projects and subsequent Klapper projects by saying, "Prior to Klapper, the work would have been developed at a much slower pace, the noise around what other issues the staff were working on would have created the potential for things to not be as thoughtfully analyzed as they were, and the result might not have been as solidly received. And that would likely have led to either delayed success, or less success...or maybe even no success."

Morning of Day Two—Starting to Apply Your New Perspective

We're all rested after a challenging day. Many of us are having our second cup of coffee as we kick off day two. We reassign positions so people have a chance to experience the company from different perspectives and we jump in, beginning to utilize some of the lessons learned yesterday afternoon.

In their new roles, with some new skills under their belts, participants drive NAVCorp toward a few improvements. Now, NAVCorp is stable, although its operations are still suboptimal. Silos still exist and there continue to be conflicting goals and measures, yet management is beginning to understand the process concept and how the enterprise can use it to improve overall performance. They have identified and documented some, but not all, business processes. Unlike yesterday, employees realize that the purpose of their work is to deliver exceptional customer value. And frontline workers begin to stretch their performance goals to align with company objectives.

Employees experience how optimizing department-level performance without building connections across the organization doesn't deliver desired results. They feel the impact of internal focus versus customer focus. They realize how bureaucracy inhibits a quick response to changing market conditions and discover how hierarchical decision-making contributes to slowed actions. Finally, they draw profound connections between NAVCorp and their own organization.

Overall, it's a bit better. But it's not great.

After fiscal year 2 ends, we once again sit down at the table in the debriefing section of our 1600 square feet of space. We now apply the Results Triangle in a formal, fact-based approach to the organization.

Afternoon of Day Two—Crossing the Threshold of Greatness

Over the past day and a half, the participants have led a three-year, organization-wide transformation. But something new is in the air. Participants are excited about what comes next. They volunteer for new positions and begin working at NAVCorp, fiscal year 3.

As the afternoon unfolds, I make a number of observations. I note that the senior management team has a clear understanding of and aggressively pursues the company strategy, and they view transformation not as a singular event but as an objective to pursue on an ongoing basis. I also note that participants exhibit a passion for execution excellence, operating in a customer-centered organization with clearly defined and understood measures and optimized organizational performance. Fact-based decisions are made authoritatively— by frontline personnel. What a difference from yesterday.

Partnerships with customers and vendors are now part of NAVCorp's normal way of doing business. Associates recognize that change is inevitable and embrace it as an ongoing part of their professional life. Process owners work with their colleagues in customer and vendor organizations to drive inter-enterprise optimization.

As a result, NAVCorp's financial, operational, and cultural performance gains are dramatic, and participants are more willing to work cross-functionally to solve problems, replacing the mentality of "blame the person" with "fix the process."

All the way down to a palpable change in the participants' attitudes, the transformation from yesterday morning is profound, for me and for them. With The Corporate Lab experience, participants have made a fundamental cultural shift. They have also internalized the Results Triangle and are now ready to enthusiastically apply it to an opportunity within their own company. Both culture and process are now aligned toward a common goal of embracing change.

Benefits Following The Corporate Lab

Senior management says...	Client associates say...
"I think it was critical that our leadership team went through The Corporate Lab together."	"I can't wait to get started tomorrow [on the project in our organization]."
"It has become much clearer what I personally need to do to transform the organization."	"I always thought I knew what the answers were, but was never given the chance or the time to try."
"It was sobering to learn that 85 percent of my time as CFO is spent on non-value-added activities."	"I am flattered that management chose me for this very important task. I guess they really do want to hear what I think."
"Trusting those at every level of the organization will free up my time to spend on propelling this company forward."	"I never want to go back to working in a company like NAVCorp fiscal year 1."
"I can't believe that my usual approach is exactly the opposite of what's needed to motivate my people."	"So that's what management meant by 'distributed leadership.'"
"It's liberating to know that if I empower my front line, they'll make the right decisions."	"If we can fix NAVCorp, I have no doubt we will be successful in our company."

Right after the lab, participants feel an accelerated sense of owner-ship, passion, and enthusiasm for the adoption and execution of corporate strategy and transformative change. And because the Lab helps partici-pants internalize a set of useful scientific methods, they are now ready to enthusiastically apply them throughout the organization and function at a higher level than ever before. The team, now sharing a common experience and common language, can also utilize more relevant inputs to inform their problem solving. In addition, the team shares a common analytic toolbox to approach the transformation that they are about to embark on, which will result in richer solutions.

One of the greatest benefits of the Lab is that its impact remains long after the Lab ends. It continues to help the leadership team create a com-pelling story and understand how to lead a transformation. It continues to generate ongoing meaningful results throughout future transformation projects. And it enables everyone to think in a creative way as the key con-cepts, phrases, and metaphors from the Lab interweave into the fabric of the organization. Even after the initial change project is achieved—to be

discussed more in the next chapter—the Lab will continue to inspire you to take on substantial, enterprise-wide change as you continue to see that achieving such transformation is doable. In fact, it's where the real work begins.

A Few Additional Exercises

Behavioral change isn't easy for most adults. Lectures, training programs, and workshops can explain the intellectual elements of transformation, but they are seldom effective at getting to the behavioral aspects that lie at the heart of a significant change initiative. Further, under normal working conditions, managers are often too busy to offer up the resources necessary to pursue lasting change.

After reading about the experience offered by The Corporate Lab, I hope that you can see the profound effect two days can have on a small but powerful force. Although The Corporate Lab can't be replaced, there are some effective exercises that can help you change the mind-set and behaviors within your organization.

Of the many that I have studied, witnessed, and employed, the following three—Don't Touch Me, the Marshmallow Challenge, and the Tennis Ball Exercise—have repeatedly yielded the most consequential results. They do have a gamelike air about them, which means that participants will not take them as seriously, and they will not instantly and directly connect the learning back to the organization, but there is still a great deal of value in them and I recommend that you consider using these exercises.

Don't Touch Me

This exercise is useful for distinguishing between continuous improvement and breakthrough improvement. It can also promote deeper thought and more substantive discussions about how our perceptions and assumptions can limit our choices.

Group Size/Configuration

Almost any size group from ten to a hundred can work. You will need a facilitator. If the group has an odd number of participants, then the facilitator will need to participate as someone's partner.

Space/Supplies Needed

You will need a room that is large enough to accommodate the group, with room to move around. You'll need a timer or a clock with a second hand. You will also need one small, sturdy object. You can use almost anything, from a soccer ball to a dog collar to a clock radio. The object should be set on a chair or on the floor, and there should be enough space for the entire group to circle around it.

The Task

Each member of the group will need to touch the object as quickly as possible, subject to certain constrictions, to be explained. The event is timed. Each group tries several times to achieve what the facilitator will tell them is world-class performance.

Directions and Facilitator Script

1. Welcome to ABC Incorporated. Would each person please grab a partner and line up beside that partner in the circle?
2. Your goal is for each person on the team to touch the object and then switch places with his or her partner. Because we at ABC Inc. are so safety conscious, we're going to require that no one make any physical contact whatsoever with anyone else for the duration of the attempt, and that each person repeat the company's OSHA-approved safety mantra: "Don't Touch Me!"
3. I'll give you a few minutes to plan your strategy, and then signal for you to begin. I'll be timing you from the moment you begin until the task is completed. If anyone touches anyone else on the team, a penalty of five seconds per touch will be added to your time.
4. After we assess a time, you will have more time to plan, and will get another chance to attempt the task and lower your time. Any questions?

Facilitator Notes

1. Some person or persons will be unclear from the start about the task. Whenever someone asks "What are we doing?" say the following: "Let me repeat the specifications. Each person on the team must touch the object. Each person on the team must NOT touch anyone else. Each person on the team must switch places with his or her partner. Each person must repeat the safety mantra, 'Don't Touch Me.'" I suggest that you say it just as written because you are trying to give instructions that are clear and don't mislead the participants yet don't give too much away.
2. First attempts are often very long (say two to three seconds for each person in the group), there are several touches, general confusion. On the second attempt, the group will usually have defined some type of system that involves each person in the group doing the task in turn;

i.e., I and my partner each move to the center of the circle, touch the object without touching one another, then carefully move to the outside of the circle again. Then you and your partner do the same steps, then the next pair, and so on, until everyone has completed the task.

3. Third (and sometimes fourth and fifth and so on) attempts will have the group fine-tuning its approach, its organization, and process. Progress—that is, shortening the time it takes to complete each attempt—will be incremental.

4. When the group starts questioning its assumptions, it will take huge leaps forward. Someone in the group will ask you, "Do we have to stay in a circle?" You respond (per point 1 above), "Let me repeat the specifications…" But the real answer (that the group should come to without you telling them) is no, the group can start in any shape or configuration it desires. Then someone else will ask, "Do we have to start across from our partners?" Again, you repeat the specifications, but as they listen closely they will realize that there is no particular rule about where each person starts relative to her partner. Some groups even begin to question the meaning of the term "switch places." It is open for discussion, and you can be as free here as you wish.

5. "World-class performance" is, obviously, whatever you say it is—perhaps ten seconds, but you can decide the number based on the group. If your goals center around thinking outside of the box, breaking old paradigms, etc., you may at some point casually mention that your biggest competitor, XYZ Incorporated, was recently clocked at 1.2 seconds. This will intensify the questioning and reexamining of the process that I point out in step 4. A "world-class" solution usually involves a reconfiguring of the group so that partners are right next to each other and simultaneous movement of one half of the group immediately followed by the simultaneous movement of the other half.

The Marshmallow Challenge

This challenge was invented by Peter Skillman of Palm, Inc. and popularized by Tom Wujec of Autodesk.[3]

The goal sounds simple but it's surprisingly difficult—and revealing. In just eighteen minutes, teams of four must build the tallest freestanding structure they can out of twenty sticks of spaghetti, one yard of tape, one yard of string, and a single marshmallow. One twist is that the marshmallow has to be on top.

The task forces people to collaborate quickly. It also teaches that prototyping matters, that diverse skills matter, and that incentives magnify outcomes. One of the great things about the marshmallow challenge is that it provides teams with a shared felt experience, a common language, and a solid stance to find the right prototypes to build their real projects successfully.

I strongly encourage you to visit *marshmallowchallenge.com* to learn more and to set up this experiment within your own organization with your team of heroes.

Tennis Ball Exercise

This exercise can help a group develop new processes and discover new ways of looking at an existing problem. It's rather simple but effective.

Begin by having a group stand around a conference room. Keep the number reasonably small, but just about any number can work. For this example, I'll use six. Give a tennis ball to one participant and instruct him to toss it to someone else. The second person has to toss it again, but this time to someone who hasn't touched it before. Keep going until the sixth person has the ball. Then do it again, in the same order. A process has emerged. The tennis ball has to be touched by each person, in the order established by the first set of tosses, and that order cannot be changed.

Now comes the time to shake it up.

Give three tennis balls to the first person and ask him to send each one through the same process, one after another. Time the effort. Let's say it takes ten seconds.

Next, ask the group to significantly reduce the time it takes for three balls to go through the process. Inform them that they need to maintain the order but that they can change the process in other ways. Participants will likely begin to rearrange themselves so that, instead of standing on opposite sides of the room, they're in a line in the order they need to maintain. Now the process might take four seconds.

Tell them it's still not good enough.

Watch as the participants try different approaches. Once when I conducted this exercise, participants formed a tight circle, their hands in the center, so that the first person could simply drop the balls, having them roll down the hands, touching each person in order. By the end, cycle time was reduced to one second.

They came up with the process themselves, which is in many respects what this book is all about: getting those directly involved with a process to creatively come up with improvement ideas while managers get out of the way.

CHAPTER 5 TAKEAWAY

To achieve success, you must build a transformation program that allows change to be rapidly pulled across departments and throughout layers. Unless well-respected thought leaders at all levels embrace the change, the initiative will wither and eventually die.

To create widespread passion, the workforce must be exposed to *what could be*, which will let them rethink their mental models, break free from their entrenched paradigms, and embrace the opportunity to learn.

The Corporate Lab drives the ability to produce lasting change around the Q-Loop. It has redefined the mind-set and cultural attitudes of hundreds of organizations.

The Lab absorbs the cultural norms of an organization, which lets participants view familiar information through a very different lens. This new way of viewing their organization and themselves recalibrates their perspective and makes them open to change.

There are some effective exercises that can help you further change the mind-set and behaviors within your organization, including Don't Touch Me, the Marshmallow Challenge, and the Tennis Ball Exercise.

COMING UP

You will now take the lessons learned about shifting your organization's mind-set and apply them to the mandate you selected in chapter 4. You will also learn a proven scientific method developed by The Klapper Institute and apply it to your mandate. Using your team of heroes, you will create a prototype that you will fully embed into your organization quicker than you might think possible.

6

A Scientific Method for Achieving Your Mandate

I saw the angel in the marble and carved until I set him free.

—MICHELANGELO

All points are easy to understand once they are discovered; the point is to discover them.

—GALILEO GALILEI

After most two-day Corporate Lab experiences, I have the pleasure on the second evening of going out to dinner with all the participants. It's great to see them in a different, more relaxed setting, where we can celebrate their transformation into a high-performing team capable of evolving NAVCorp into a world-class organization. And it's great to keep the conversation and energy going. Momentum is key after the Lab. After all, these aren't the kind of people who like to wait around for results. They get frustrated and bored—and if that happens, they might start to doubt that they can get where they want to go.

I wish I could talk directly with you about your mandate, your team of heroes, and what you think about The Corporate Lab experience. I would like little more than to hear whether you employed any of the exercises included in the last chapter, or what other methods you used to kindle a mind-set–shifting transformation among your team. I do hope you now have a better understanding of your organization and the choices you make when confronted with certain scenarios, challenges, and decisions. I also hope you can approach solutions differently within your organization and are ready to pursue the mandate you selected back in chapter 4. Here's my challenge to you now: I want you to create a fully operational prototype within thirty days. Sound naively optimistic? It's really not.

I believe that you—because of the methods I'll share with you in this chapter and the intensive self-examination you did in the last chapter—will be prepared to achieve it. On top of that, I know how essential it is that you strike quickly and boldly with your ambitious mandate and newly inspired team to achieve real change. Otherwise they, and even you, will come to believe this initiative will fizzle like so many others.

Back in chapter 4, you laid the groundwork for this chapter. As a quick review, here are the nine steps you completed to pave the way for delivering your mandate:

DID YOU KNOW?

Early in 2012, builders in China spent just fifteen days constructing a thirty-story prefabricated hotel. Modules were built in a factory and then bolted together at the construction site. If you think it sounds flimsy, consider that it can reportedly withstand a 9.0-magnitude earthquake.[1]

1. Ensure senior management support
2. Choose the project
3. Select the project champion
4. Scope the work
5. Write the mandate
6. Select the coach
7. Select the team leader
8. Select the team members
9. Secure dedicated team space and team requirements

Assuming you have all of these steps in place, let's now begin the job of achieving your mandate in less than thirty days.

A True Story

Let me share a story as you kick off this phase of the Q-Loop. Several years ago, I ran The Corporate Lab for a large national insurance company. At the time, this company was taking far too long to respond to companies' requests for customized pricing information on specific insurance products. It took this prominent insurance company an average of 183 days to respond to such requests. Expecting companies to wait half a year for a price quote was hurting business. Not surprisingly, the mandate we chose was to get the response rate to less than thirty days, so that this organization could call itself an industry leader.

We ran The Corporate Lab on a Monday and Tuesday to prepare the team of heroes for this challenging mandate. It went great. Yet, as we kicked off the change initiative, I noted that there was an unexpected air of malaise among the team. Over the next two days, I deduced the reason. The team just wasn't inspired enough by the mandate.

Sure, going from 183 days to less than thirty would be an important accomplishment, but once we started to analyze the mandate and use the tools we'd learned in The Corporate Lab, the team could easily see how we could accomplish this feat: shave off twenty days here, slice off thirty days there, and so on. It got me thinking…

For lunch on Friday afternoon, the product champion and I met, just the two of us. She was a senior executive at the organization who had brought me in for this project. I said to her, "I think we need to recalibrate the mandate to shake things up."

She was open to it and asked what I had in mind, not expecting my next two words.

"One day," I said.

Her face told the story. Clearly, she thought I was crazy.

I justified my position by saying that the team needed a real jolt. There's a small risk that it will momentarily demoralize them, I told her, by making them feel they won't be able to accomplish such a brazen challenge. I added, "But I think in short order it will become exactly what we need."

From a business perspective, a response time of one day would put this organization on the leading edge. From a transformation perspective, it would underscore everything we'd been talking about and could transfigure this organization forever. We agreed that a single day might be out of reach—but not necessarily—and there was value in giving it a try.

At the end of that Friday, we called a quick meeting before everyone went home. Reentering what we had christened the war room, the project champion looked around at the faces, paused for a few moments, and then told them that she had ever-so-slightly tweaked the mandate. I thought, *Ever so slightly my foot.*

"We decided that we are going to reduce the response rate from our current average of 183 days down to a single day," she said.

No one moved. No one spoke.

Then the team leader politely said that they all needed to digest this news over the weekend. Under the surface, though, the project champion and I sensed skepticism and frustration as participants left the room. I heard someone say something about them all going to a nearby bar for a drink. Someone else seconded the idea. Although I wasn't invited, and neither was the project champion, the team evidently felt that a few drinks would help lubricate their digestion.

Monday morning, the team came back and said, "We're ready. Let's get going."

Apparently, Friday evening's mini-binge was the final push they needed to go from fear to fervor, from panic to passion. Within two-and-a-half weeks of that moment, the team had a pilot up and running in which they got the price quote response rate down from 183 days to under twenty-four hours. And they did it by discovering the answers already there before them, albeit buried beneath the 183-day morass of their previous approach. They did it by completely discarding the old way and by being given permission to risk failure, to use their collective smarts. And they did it by applying the skills they learned in The Corporate Lab, which they were already beginning to make their own.

I share this story not only because it shows how important it is to select an inspirational mandate, but because it demonstrates how important it is to truly crush your paradigm—to stop trying to improve the old ways and instead develop an entirely new way of looking at a situation.

Project Launch Day

This is an essential day, and so structuring the time in a meaningful way is important to ensure a solid foundation for the project to come. The following steps have been road-tested and will help you create the most productive first day possible.

Opening Remarks (Thirty Minutes)

Coming into the first meeting following The Corporate Lab experience, the team members (whom you selected via the process outlined in chapter 4) generally feel a hodgepodge of turbulent emotions—excitement, anxiety, fatigue. Sometimes members even feel unworthy of having been selected for the team, though the assignment should be viewed as prestigious. It's therefore important to remind participants why they were selected.

They're the real heroes of your organization, high-value players who understand how to get work done, even if they don't always do it precisely according to the rules (not to say they're rule breakers, just occasional rule benders). They are the influencers to whom fellow employees turn with questions. They are leaders—even if their titles don't always reflect it—who will help to drive this change initiative to success. One thing I consistently tell team members is that they were chosen because, paradoxically, they're the employees the organization can least afford to go without during their time commitment on this project. It's a good segue into discussing how much of their time will be required for the project, which, in turn, offers an opportunity to discuss the next topic.

It's imperative that team members know at the outset of the project that, although the work is imposing, they will have a tremendous amount of organizational support in terms of both time and resources. In addition, assure them that there will be a strong fact-based approach used, which we will learn later in this chapter. Having such a productive initial conversation is a great way to get the team off to a strong start and to ease many of their fears.

The ideal person to deliver these messages is the project champion, that senior management person you selected in chapter 4 to serve as the organization's representative. This person's job is to let the team members know that they have management's full support. The second-best option is the coach, also identified in chapter 4.

You should then formally present the mandate. Keep it simple and clear. Answer questions, but don't get sidetracked by minute details. They can be dealt with later. Just be sure everyone understands the essentials of the project.

Note that all of this should be covered in just thirty minutes. These opening remarks should be brisk and targeted, to send the unmistakable message to all that time will not be wasted at any point during this project.

Assigning Team Roles (Thirty Minutes)

Begin by naming the team leader of the group, who was selected using the guidelines laid out in chapter 4. Use your judgment to decide whether this individual should have already been informed of the decision or whether now is the right time to make the announcement. Because the team leader is just being introduced to the process, the coach generally facilitates the rest of the first-day meeting. Starting at the next meeting, the team leader takes over.

There are four additional roles that need to be named, in addition to the project champion, the coach, and the team leader. These are the commitment tracker, the timekeeper, the team historian, and the scribe.

The *commitment tracker* ensures that the responsibilities of each team member are recorded in a detailed manner and that they are achieved on time. This person will create and maintain a database of all commitments made by team members at every meeting, and at the close of each meeting will read aloud the list of commitments, the team member responsible, and the due date for each action. Then, at the opening of each meeting, this person should read aloud all open commitments, the team member responsible, and the due date for each action. As team members provide progress reports regarding their responsibilities, the commitment tracker updates the list. Key skills for this role are great organizational skills, thoroughness, and enough backbone to bluntly state if anyone is lagging behind on responsibilities.

The *team historian* maintains records of all key data, actions, and issues that arise during meetings. These records can be handwritten or typed (a better option for sharing among team members). Using a recording device in the room is also an option. Of course, no one wants or needs to listen again to five hours of meetings, but written notes can be used to capture key events with a time stamp written down to indicate key decision points or insights for later review.

The *timekeeper* ensures that meetings have formal agendas and are run efficiently. This person needs to be capable of shepherding less relevant conversations back on track and keeping meetings focused on the most salient points. The timekeeper should use a stopwatch to ensure that each topic on the agenda is performed within the time allotted by the team leader.

The *scribe* records ideas and major decisions on a flip chart during the team meetings. This role is different from the team historian in that it is more front and center. This person should have legible handwriting and be able to stand in front of the group to capture key moments in clear, spare language. This person might need to ask for clarification and must be able to rephrase ideas.

If the team is larger than five people, then those extra members will not be required to perform an extra duty, or you might choose to assign them another role that makes sense for your team. Please note that there are only five additional responsibilities assigned to the team members (the coach and the project champion roles are not fulfilled by the team itself).

Selecting a Team Name (Fifteen Minutes)

The next activity on day one is always a rousing one, and it's the first opportunity for the scribe to put marker to flip chart and record ideas and decisions. This step is deciding on a team tame. Don't think this is a frivolous exercise. A team name provides the team with an important sense of unity and identity, and it communicates objectives and influences perception. It will bring you all together under one umbrella and it will also create a convenient way to refer to the group.

Naming is hard, but for this exercise you don't need to worry about trademarks and available domains and all the other things that make full-on naming projects so difficult. Keep it loose and fun and come up with something memorable. For this purpose, the best names are directly related to the mandate.

Here are some actual examples of effective team names from clients I've worked with:

- Scratch and Dent Detectives
- FAST (Fixing All Service Troubles)
- ESP (Errors Stop Pronto)
- Red Tape Busters
- Paper Chasers

Within fifteen short minutes, decide on your name. If you want to change it later, fine. Certainly, you can go into the meeting with some ideas for a team name, but it's better to do this activity on the spot and do it quickly so that everyone feels like he is part of the process and so that it best serves its purpose, which is to help the team coalesce around the mandate.

DID YOU KNOW?

FedEx Take a look at the space between the "E" and the "x" in the FedEx logo. This arrow is meant to communicate speed and precision, fundamental elements of the FedEx brand.[2]

amazon.com The arrow in Amazon's logo is more than a decorative flourish. It signifies that Amazon sells everything from A to Z and also imitates the smile on customers' faces when they receive their products.[3]

A team logo is also helpful and fun, and can be used on team correspondence, presentations, and agendas. Some clients have shirts printed with the team name and logo, which the team wears proudly on Fridays to communicate to the rest of the organization that they're on a special project.

Developing Team Ground Rules (Thirty Minutes)

Ground rules help team members understand how they are expected to behave during the entire project. They also provide for a more disciplined approach to team development. The scribe records these rules on a flip chart, and the rules should be hung front and center in the room and remain there for the duration of the project.

Most of the team members will have had experience with other teams—some positive and others not so positive—and it's useful for members to bring this experience to the current team as they create the list of ground rules. A positive exercise is to take ten minutes for each member to write down both the negative and positive attributes of past teams, then discuss the results for five minutes. From this exercise, begin to suggest a list of ten commandments for the team. Stay focused on the core goal of the project.

Some potential ground rules might include:

- Each member must attend all meetings unless excused by other members
- All meetings start and end on time
- Everyone has an equal voice
- Blame the process, not the people
- Late arrivals must bring donuts to the next meeting
- The team will follow the Results Triangle
- Don't jump to solutions

What other rules might work for you?

Understanding the Happy Curve™ (Five Minutes)

Please, don't be intimidated by this complex chart. After all, I do have an MBA from the Wharton School of Business. But seriously folks...The Happy Curve is a fun and meaningful way to introduce the concept of the emotional roller coaster that teams will experience during this project.

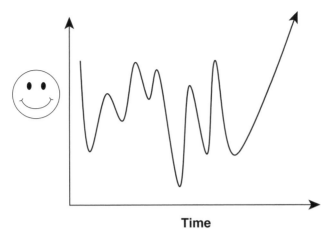

Figure 6-1: The Happy Curve™

Better to discuss the ups and downs of the project ahead of time than have to deal with them in the moment. Having this conversation early assures team members that you understand and can empathize with their emotional journey.

When I coach projects, I begin each meeting by asking, "Where's everyone on the Happy Curve today?" It proves to be a humorous and empathic way to take the group's temperature and address challenges as proactively as possible.

In my experience, most people coming into the project feel like they rank somewhere around an 8 on a scale of 1 to 10, with 10 being excellent. Pretty soon into day one, however, they hear the challenging mandate and they drop down to about a 4 or 5. Then they discuss the mandate, pick a team name, and start to get excited, and they're back up to a 7. From week to week, day to day, even hour to hour, the group will fluctuate. Interestingly, although there will be some deviation among team members, it's usually slight, as a team mind-set kicks in and members share thoughts, frustrations, and accomplishments.

Another thing to keep in mind is that at the end of the project, most teams rank their emotions around a 9 or 10 on the Happy Curve.

Discussing the Project Time Line (Fifteen Minutes)

If the project mandate is properly focused and the team is composed of dedicated, high-potential members, the project will be completed through prototyping within four weeks. Be sure you understand the following time line fully before reviewing it with the team. When you do review it with the team, keep the summary brief, assuring the team that you will detail each step of the process during the remainder of today's meeting and will pick up where you leave off tomorrow.

Week One will be spent listening to the voice of the customer through customer surveys, as well as listening to the voice of the business by collecting and verifying baseline performance measures, mapping the process, and performing strategy, organization, or process analyses.

Week Two will be spent developing a hypothesis for a root cause analysis, performing a root cause analysis, and selecting candidates for experiments. During this week, the team might begin to design initial experiments as well.

Week Three will continue with conducting experiments and monitoring them (ideally, there will be several experiments running in parallel). This week will culminate in the team combining all experiments into a pilot, which the team will prepare to launch in the final week.

Week Four will involve the team launching the pilot, monitoring the pilot, and modifying it as needed. The team will also develop a detailed implementation plan during this fourth week.

After discussing the project time line, you might find that the team is down a few pegs on the Happy Curve. No worries; it's natural. The upcoming sections will give the team the boost they need.

Brainstorming Baseline Performance Measures (Sixty Minutes)

The key baseline performance measures (BPM) represent the health of the particular operation related to your mandate. It's smart to brainstorm and agree on what these measures are on the first day of the project to create a snapshot of precisely where you are today. This exercise creates a baseline against which you can measure where you are going to be tomorrow and all of the changes that will be required to get there. At the end of the project, these same measures can be used to create a compelling before-and-after picture. Approximately six to ten measures should be identified.

If your mandate concerns something that is currently unprofitable, then consider what measures and dimensions of profitability are relevant.

If the mandate concerns something process related, then what are the current measures of quality or time or cost? In other words, what is the before picture you are dealing with and what are the ten quantitative BPMs that define what this before scenario looks like? Note my use of the word *quantitative*. For a BPM to have any value, there must be a way to define and accurately measure it.

Don't worry at first about coming up with too many measures. You'll start to see some redundancy and will note that some measures can be replaced by others. In the end, the scribe should record the ten agreed-upon measures on a flip chart.

Consider using some version of the following table format, and record the measures in the left column. This shows the future-oriented focus of the project and will help to document your progression. On this first day, you should at least complete the first column of the following chart. Clearly, the third and fourth columns can't be completed until the project progresses. The second column may not be completed within the time allotted on day one, and if it's not, assign appropriate team members to complete the assessment of the current environment for day two.

Baseline Performance Measures	Current Environment	New Environment	Percentage Improvement

It's important to note that using self-stick paper flip charts with a flip chart easel is an excellent way to document your progress and demonstrate to outsiders how much work you are actually doing. One consistent experience among my many project teams concerns the reaction of people from outside the team: when these colleagues come into the war room, they typically declare some variation of "I can't believe how much work you've done in such a short time!" Hearing such praise gives everyone on the team a real boost.

Learning the Results Triangle (Two Hours)

I offer the full details of the Results Triangle beginning on page 139, where it makes sense for this book. Feel free to skip forward now to read about the Results Triangle.

Commitment Tracker End-of-Day Review (Five Minutes)

At the end of day one, and at the end of every meeting until the conclusion of the project, ask the commitment tracker to review all of the items that individual team members have been assigned by stating the team member's name, the commitment made to the team, and the due date. The commitment tracker should also lead off each team meeting by reading aloud all commitments and determining whether the responsible team member has performed the task.

Preparing for Future Meetings

Different approaches to the way meetings are conducted produce different behavior patterns and results. Many team leaders make the mistake of conducting all meetings in the same way. It's important to understand the objective of each meeting prior to the start to ensure an effective outcome.

Team leaders sometimes make the mistake of focusing too much attention on the strict use of time, for example. When the primary purpose of the meeting is to share information, review progress, or make decisions, the time-efficient approach makes sense. But this approach doesn't work so well when the team needs to perform real work that goes beyond progress reviews and approvals. Problem solving should have an open-ended time frame and these types of meetings should be run much more loosely than a rigid agenda allows. An effective team leader uses different approaches, depending on the outcome desired.

The team leader should consider what the team needs to deliver by the end of the meeting, which team members need to contribute to accomplish these deliverables, and what kinds of contributions should be expected from various participants. The team leader should also assess whether there will likely be resistance or obstacles. If attempts are made to divert the meeting from its primary purpose, the team leader must determine how to handle it. Other questions for the team leader include who should lead the overall meeting, who should lead the work on a particular topic, whether the team should divide into subgroups and, if so, the purpose for the subgroup discussion.

The Results Triangle

I've tested your patience long enough. Now it's time to learn the Results Triangle, which comprises three powerful steps designed for you to systematically and consistently deliver on the promises made to your customers.

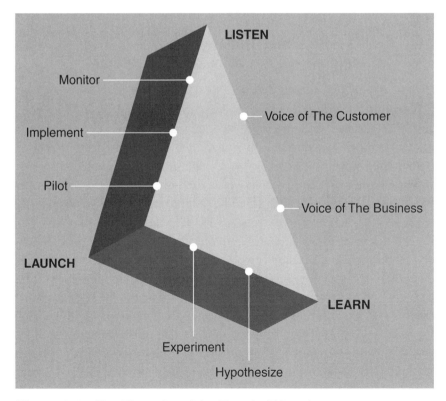

Figure 6-2: The Three Ls of the Results Triangle

The three Ls of the Results Triangle are:

Listen—Listen to both the customer and the business by interviewing customers and key stakeholders, analyzing past research and documents, assessing competitor positioning, and mapping key processes.

Learn—Learning is the act of understanding the current operating environment, analyzing its performance, hypothesizing potential root causes, and conducting experiments to validate the hypotheses.

Launch—Launching initially begins with a series of rapid prototypes or pilots, followed by a carefully coordinated rollout and detailed monitoring.

Listen Phase—Step 1
Listening to the Voice of the Customer

If you are truly interested in achieving breakthrough performance gains, it is essential to understand—at a deep and profound level—how your customer behaves. In doing so, it becomes clear how you can tailor your products and service offerings to exceed their desires. By delighting your customers, you will create loyalty, you will profit, and you will distinguish yourself from your competitors—providing that you learn to perform astute customer-focused analysis and continue to perform it in an ongoing fashion.

The customer must be considered at the start of all major change initiatives. Learning to listen to the customer will help you identify the specific customer needs around which a product or business process will be designed, or understand how customer needs relate to strategy development, growth, achieving operational excellence, or preparing for an IT implementation. Learning to listen to the voice of the customer will let you establish clear standards of performance based on actual customer input. It will also help you obtain a complete description of the factors that create customer satisfaction, including output requirements and service requirements.

As I mentioned in chapter 5, no question generates more debate (at least for many organizations) than "Who is your customer?" My experience is that, often, organizations struggle to identify who their customer really is. I agree with Sam Walton's perspective: "There is only one boss. The customer. And he can fire everybody in the company from the chairman on down, simply by spending his money elsewhere."

Do you agree with Sam Walton too? Does your organization have consensus regarding who your customer is? I make no bones about it: I am assertive about my position that your customers are the ones who pay your bills. Period. I hope you agree. If not, or if other team members do not agree, spend at least a few minutes with the team having a discussion about who your customer really is.

> **DID YOU KNOW?**
>
> Amazon founder and CEO Jeff Bezos sometimes leaves an empty seat at a conference table and tells attendees that the seat is occupied by their customer, "the most important person in the room."[4]

Once you have accurately identified who your customers are—and only then—you are ready to speak with them directly to find out what they value.

Creating a Customer Survey

I have been associated with organizations that have spent millions of dollars and many months surveying their customers. I take a radically different approach. And it has served me extremely well over the years. I call my survey strategy the Rule of 10^3 (pronounced "ten cubed").

Rule of 10^3 means ten questions, conducted with ten customers, prepared and launched in ten hours. For the focused work that you are performing, if you can ask the precisely targeted ten questions to the right ten customers, you will learn 90 percent of what you need to know and then move to the next step of the Results Triangle. If you have the right people on your team, developing and completing the survey should take no more than ten hours.

Rule of 10^3 surveys might include the following key questions:

- What products or services do you buy from us?
- How are you using what we provide?
- What do you value most?
- What do you need?

- Why do you need it that way?
- How do you measure your needs?
- Are we meeting your needs?
- Which ones are falling short?
- What is your number one source of dissatisfaction?
- How do you prioritize your unmet needs?

Because customers don't always know what they don't know, it's critical to follow each question with "Why?" and "Why not?" prompts.

Conducting a Customer Survey

Once a punchy, high-impact set of ten survey questions has been agreed upon by the team, it's time to conduct the survey with ten customers. Ideally, surveys should be conducted by two team members with one customer at a time, although multiple surveys can be conducted simultaneously by separate pairs of team members.

A solid approach is for one team member to take the lead in asking questions while the other focuses on recording the answers accurately and asking follow-up questions if necessary. Conducting surveys over the phone is fine. Face-to-face sessions are preferable if it's convenient, though often it's not. E-mail surveys should be an absolute last resort, as the answers are less reliable and less robust.

> ── **DID YOU KNOW?** ──
>
> Up to 96 percent of unhappy customers don't complain. However, 91 percent of those unhappy customers will leave and not come back. Typical dissatisfied customers tell between nine and fifteen people about their experience, but happy customers who get their issue resolved tell only four to six people about their experience.[5]

After the Rule of 10^3 surveys are completed, which should occur by the end of week one or the first half of week two, it's time to write an issue statement from the findings. An issue statement is a clear, concise description of the key issue that your mandate needs to address based on the feedback you receive from customers. This statement is used to focus the team at the start of the process, keep the team on track during the effort, and validate that the effort has delivered an outcome that solves the key issue. The issue statement will provide focus and discipline for the team's thought process and strategy throughout the project.

The survey results provide the team with the customer's perspective on what is needed to solve the mandated issue. It can also be used to verify the mandate and provide clarity. For example, if the mandate is to "grow business by increasing sales to current customers," a portion of the survey should ask the following questions:

- What products/services are you currently purchasing from our company?
- Have you considered purchasing additional products/services from our company?
- If you have not considered purchasing additional products/services, why not? (Please be specific.)
- What would it take for you to consider purchasing additional products/services? (Please be specific.)

Listen Phase—Step 2
Listening to the Voice of the Business

Listening to the voice of the business means generating a deep and thorough understanding of how the business is performing today. If you want to focus on strategy, then you must be sure decision makers have a solid understanding of the business, its strategy, and the assumptions behind that strategy. You should determine who should attend strategic planning sessions (six to eight people usually works best, and these should all be key decision makers).

Be careful, because everyone will want to attend, but *contributing* to strategic planning is different from merely *attending* the meetings. Be sure to set aside time on the calendars for this important undertaking—typically, about twenty business days during the year should be spent on strategic planning for the company.

Make sure data is available in advance of the meeting (including customer trends, competitor analysis, operational assessment, economics, and key people issues for all relevant segments of the business).

If you are focused on operational improvement instead of strategy, then use the process mapping discussed in chapter 4, where I outlined process mapping as one of the necessary steps prior to assembling the team and writing the mandate. Now, you'll take that initial process map that you created to the next level and involve all members of the team.

As I mentioned before, process mapping is the technique of using flow-charts to illustrate the flow of a process. The process map that you will be creating during this part of the Results Triangle will proceed from the most macro perspective to the level of detail required to identify opportunities for improvement. Process mapping focuses on the work rather than on job titles or hierarchy. A proper process map will let the team picture the work itself, not the organization.

I have seen process mapping take months. Perhaps you have too. At the Klapper Institute, we use what we call Rapid Process Mapping (RPM). The principle of RPM is that we only map what needs to be documented, which eliminates most of the time spent mapping a process. If done properly, with the appropriate people involved, RPM should take about an hour.

An RPM process map should have no more than eight steps and should always begin and end with the customer. Starting with the macro view will enable you to get a comprehensive view of the entire operation that you are examining.

Once you have mapped the macro process, use the issue statement to determine where in the process you should drill down to gain additional insight. For example, if the issue is that the cost of the operation is too high (a directive that would likely come from the mandate, not the customer), rather than examining how you could make each step in the process more productive, look at all macro process steps and classify them as either "value-added" or "non-value-added." I determine whether a process is value-added by checking whether it meets all three of the following criteria:

1. The activity results in a change in form or function
2. The customer wants and is willing to pay for the activity
3. It is the first time that the activity is being performed (if the activity is performed multiple times, I call that rework)

I've used this simple but powerful definition across dozens of industries. Clients have always responded favorably because it's so simple to apply and causes them to look at their business in a very different way.

One client had an interesting internal debate about whether a new quality assurance step should be considered value-added. When they applied my definition, the answer was "no," because it didn't result in a change in form or function. The contention, however, was that the QA step saved the company millions of dollars and preserved customer relation-ships because it ensured that no product left without being inspected.

My position was firm. In today's world, it may be essential for the company to implement the step, but that doesn't make it value-added. Therefore it was a candidate for elimination (provided we could redesign the process to eliminate the need for QA).

IDEAS IN ACTION

I met Mike Brothers seventeen years ago. He's an incredibly smart guy who definitely doesn't suffer fools kindly—and makes no apologies for it! I had the pleasure of working with Mike at Millstone Nuclear Power Plant, where he was the senior vice president of nuclear operations. I also had the chance to catch up with him in a conversation for this book. An exceptional leader, Mike remembers nonetheless having difficulty effecting real change at the plant.

In response, we launched a series of teams, each one with a separate and valuable mandate. Mike recalls, "Millstone was dealing with issues involving work management processes, prioritization processes, to name just some. We wanted to better focus on improving value-added activities and stop wasting time on the non-value-added stuff."

As we achieved mandate after mandate, success after success, we got to a critical mass of people thinking the way we were thinking and believing what we already knew was possible. As a result, the long-standing resistance disappeared and change swept through the organization.

Mike already knew what was possible. But making everyone else see it was hard. And that's the entire point of the way we work. It's significant that if an organization doesn't have the chance to acquire that same perspective that Mike and a series of teams developed at Millstone, it will invariably hit obstacles. Ideas simply can't be pushed in from the outside or down through the organization. They have to be pulled from the bottom.

To illustrate, compare Mike's success with the experience of another leader I spoke with recently. This leader is someone I also worked with several years ago at another company that had tremendous success working with us. He told me a story that's diametrically opposed to Mike's experience at Millstone.

(continued)

Now at a major renewable energy company, this senior leader is facing teeth-gnashing frustration trying to implement changes. He's fighting battle after battle on burdensome and frequently unnecessary documentation of compliance issues. According to this senior leader, "Instead of getting something in front of workers that's actually to the point, we're putting in front of them compliance-based documents that are fifty or sixty pages long. To think that these union guys are going to read these things . . . you're fooling yourself."

This leader went on to say that these employees just want to work. But because of the compliance-based mentality—versus a value-added point of view—tons of hurdles get in the workers' way. He added, "We have reams of requirements workers have to get through and it's mostly made up of boilerplate. So it can take a week to get through a job when it should be done in hours."

What ends up happening is that a group of people crowds around, say, a welder, telling him to hurry because he's slowing down the works. But the issue isn't that he's welding too slowly, contrary to what the team currently believes. The problem is that it took them two weeks to get all of the paperwork and approvals in the right place before that welder could do his job. People are managing what they can see instead of identifying the root cause of an inefficient process that should be streamlined—if only they could develop a method to identify it and then implement that change effectively.

The executive manager recounted in our conversation that he used to do much the same thing prior to using our approach. But then he discovered what the team of heroes was able to accomplish in a short time.

Sensing his genuine frustration, I explained that it's a Sisyphean task to have just one person who's been to the other side of the mountain trying to explain to everybody that grass is green and the valley is lush . . . just trust me! It's because they haven't been through the same sort of mind-set–shifting experience as the senior leader.

His job now is to figure out how to take them through a transformational experience much like the one described in this chapter.

Learn Phase—Step 1
Hypothesizing the Root Cause of the Problem

In the Learn phase, we begin by developing hypotheses to determine the root cause of the issue. This phase will help you to avoid a conference room solution as described in chapter 4. To help you see the dangers of a conference room solution, consider the following real scenario that I use in The Corporate Lab.

The marble of the iconic Jefferson Memorial was deteriorating. The cause was posited as too-frequent cleanings with an abrasive detergent. So what is the solution? Less frequent cleanings? A different detergent? Those are the initial answers most people give. But it turned out that cleaning wasn't the root cause of the problem, and so these weren't the optimal solutions. In fact, these misguided solutions led to other problems.

The detergent was necessary because otherwise the voluminous bird droppings from local sparrows would have built up. Finally, it was observed that the sparrows were attracted by spiders. The spiders were attracted by gnats. The gnats were attracted by lights. That's right—the true root cause of the deterioration was the lights on the monument, which came on at dusk, when gnats are active. The solution was, therefore, to turn the lights on after dark, when the gnats are not active. Problem solved, and the solution required less work by the maintenance crew, whereas the wrong solution required more work.

Asking "why" in the right way leads to new insights and innovations that can yield elegant and powerful solutions. Repeatedly asking why, as a child might, is a source of continuous self-renewal. But asking why properly is an art. Often, the person who is asked why something is as it is has a strong reaction. The question is rarely welcomed and it can be met with defensiveness and hostility. To ask why and why not about basic facts violates the social convention that expertise is to be respected, not challenged. Functional organizations in mature industries most certainly have this issue.

Yet this type of thoughtful probing can result in revolutionary new thoughts in quite unexpected places. Consider doctors in the early nineteenth century, who routinely went from conducting autopsies to treating patients without washing—leading to disastrous results for their patients. Ignaz Semmelweis first hypothesized a connection between hand disinfection and mortality rates. He proposed that doctors wash in a chlorinated lime solution, but this was largely rejected by the medical community and he was unable to defend his position based on yet-to-be-discovered scientific evidence. Semmelweis was only vindicated by research that occurred after his death, in a psychiatric asylum of, ironically, a systemic infection.[6]

I do not doubt that you and many of your colleagues are excellent problem solvers who generate solutions daily. But if you tend to solve the same issues repeatedly, you are not getting to the true root cause. Once you do, you will never again revisit the problem. Additionally, a clear understanding of the root cause generally results in a myriad of potential solutions, and you can then pick the most elegant (such as simply keeping the lights off at dusk).

Proper Brainstorming of Root Causes

Brainstorming is an effective way to generate ideas to solve problems, make decisions, and explore improvements. In true brainstorming, it is essential that you do not interrupt the thought process. It is a creative, free-thinking activity. As ideas come to mind, they are captured without bias on your flip chart by the scribe or by some other recording device. During brainstorming, it is necessary to avoid all distractions, so phones should be shut off, the door closed, and people focused on the activity.

Approximately twenty minutes is a good amount of time, so a timer should be set and work should be done right until the end.

Begin by creating a clear issue statement for what you are exploring. Reserve all negative judgment and use others' ideas to build on. Go for absolute quantity—try to get a hundred or more ideas written down or recorded. Don't hesitate to draw pictures or diagrams if they help. Crazy ideas are often great building blocks. The team leader should facilitate the process by stopping any side conversations and ensuring that everyone is heard, that one idea at a time is presented, and that there is no negativity.

DID YOU KNOW?

Charles Barbier, a French army officer, developed a system of night writing that made use of raised dots on paper. He designed it so his soldiers could read messages in the dark. It was a good idea, but the man who saw a new use for it in 1829 changed the lives of thousands upon thousands of blind people. His name? Louis Braille.[7]

Using the Fishbone Diagram During Brainstorming

The fishbone diagram is an analysis tool that provides a systematic way of looking at effects and at the causes that create or contribute to those effects. Because of the function of the fishbone diagram, it may be referred to as a cause-and-effect diagram, although the design of the diagram looks much like the skeleton of a fish. It was created by Dr. Kaoru Ishikawa, a

Japanese quality-control statistician. The fishbone diagram assists teams in categorizing the many potential causes of problems or issues in an orderly way and helps identify root causes.

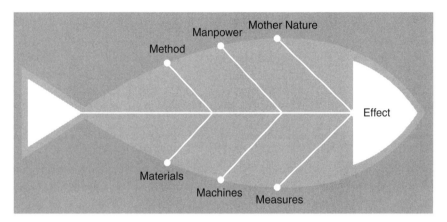

Figure 6-3: The Fishbone Diagram

Learn Phase—Step 2
Experimenting to Validate the Hypothesis

Now it's time for the team to validate the hypothesis you developed for the root cause. There are several sound principals to follow for conducting your experiments, outlined below.

Conduct Rapid and Frequent Experiments

Experiments are only effective if they deliver significant learning to the company. Although companies can save money by lumping experiments into one large test, experimenting more frequently minimizes problem-solving delays and the cost of redesign. Given that new technologies drastically reduce the cost of testing, the need for frequent experimentation becomes more vital. But companies must be prepared to handle the increased load of information that comes with greater experimentation.

DID YOU KNOW?

To prevent ideas and inspirations from growing cold, Thomas Edison based his West Orange, NJ, laboratory on the concept of rapid experimentation. Supplies and machines were close to rooms where experiments were conducted so employees' work and creativity were not hindered.[8]

Define the Objective

You should define the objective in one sentence that outlines the purpose of the experiment. It should always focus on proving or disproving a hypothesis. Experiments can be broad. For example, "The purpose of the experiment is to prove that lack of deep subject matter expertise in the relationship manager is the root cause of low follow-on sales." Or it can be very narrow: "The purpose of the experiment is to prove that lack of timely and correct initial information is the root cause of inaccurate IT forecasts."

Outline the Experiment

Write a brief two- to three-sentence description of how you will conduct the experiment. For example, "We will provide the relationship managers with deep product line information so they become true subject matter experts. Then they will use their current sales process and we will observe and calculate whether their product training has enabled them to be more effective with follow-on sales."

Determine Data to Collect

What is the critical information you need to formally collect? Data could include follow-on sales (versus control groups and versus prior performance), amount of training received, and experience levels of experiment participants, to name some possibilities.

Determine Timing and Length of Experiment

Figure out when the experiment will run and how long it will take.

Determine Roles and Responsibilities

Decide who will need to be involved and what exactly each person will do.

Fail Early and Often—but Learn from It

Novel ideas are bound to fail, which is why early failures are necessary to eliminate unfavorable options quickly and enhance learning.

Remember, experiments that result in failure are not failed experiments. Unlike mistakes, failures generate new and useful information. Embrace them.

Control Critical Variables

You cannot learn from the experiment if more than one variable is uncontrolled. Identify all of the key variables. The key variables are all the things that could impact the results of the experiment if they changed.

Modify As Necessary

Modify your experiment if all of the critical variables are not controlled or eliminated.

Experiment Checklist

Be sure to have the following in place:

- Define the objective
- Outline the experiment (just a few sentences)
- Identify all of the key variables
- Make sure all of the variables can be controlled or eliminated
- Modify as necessary
- Identify data to collect
- Determine timing and length of experiment
- Determine roles and responsibilities
- If necessary, communicate with others in the organization
- Run the experiment
- Collect data
- Learn from results
- Modify as needed

Let me give you an example of a recent experiment run by a client. The IT organization of this large financial services company was having difficulty meeting the turnaround time and quality levels demanded by their business partners for an estimating function. When the business units requested an estimate from IT for, say, a new system, function, or capability, the IT organization took about thirty days. And the actual cost proved to be plus or minus 40 percent of the estimate.

The business units were demanding an estimate within two business days and one that was plus or minus 10 percent of the actual cost. After performing all the steps within "Listen" and "Learn," the team hypothesized that, because they had nearly fifty disparate systems across the organization, more than forty IT experts were involved in every estimate—and so each estimate essentially began with a blank sheet of paper.

They developed an experiment to prove that not having a single estimator with cradle-to-grave responsibility and accountability resulted in long turnaround times and high error rates. After running the initial experiment with a senior estimator who had vast experience across many of the systems, the team learned that a single person significantly reduced the complexity and time required to deliver an accurate estimate. They also realized, however, that gaps existed between the knowledge level of even the most senior estimator and the knowledge needed to complete an estimate.

The next experiment occurred the following day. The team selected an estimate that had already been performed and provided the senior estimator with all the information that had been collected to deliver that estimate. Armed with the necessary information, the estimator was able to deliver the estimate within an hour.

The experiment was a huge success. The team realized that the root cause of the delays and inaccuracy in the estimates was that the process involved too many people and that not enough background information was being given.

But the team, of course, wasn't finished. They next needed to design a pilot based on the insights they had gained from the experiment.

Launch Phase—Step 1
Building a Pilot

Now that the experiment phase is complete and any deficiencies or customizations are addressed, it's time to launch the pilot process. It might seem counterintuitive, but to achieve your mandate it's imperative that you build a pilot that's rough, rapid, and right. In other words, it's not meant to be a finished product. Think of it as a rehearsal for the final performance—and not even the dress rehearsal. As such, the ideal pilot will take just a few days to develop and implement. Because you will learn so much from an operational pilot in the field, it's better to get the pilot started and modify from factual and observational data as you go along instead of debating the merits of specific elements beforehand.

When selecting a department to pilot, you may want to choose an area that is enthusiastic about the change, has a history of problems with the old process, and is influential in the organization. Most important, you want to ensure that the manager or managers of the pilot area are committed to it and prepared to drive the change.

Depending on your mandate, there are several types of pilots that can be mixed and matched as needed.

- Offline: not performed on actual customers/actual services, but simulated by using old customer information/requests to minimize any potential disruption to business.
- Limited duration: depending on the pilot, these can be run for a week, a month, or a quarter, but they have well-defined stop and start dates.
- Segmented customers/products: provides scope to make the pilot more manageable by operating in one customer segment (such as affluent customers) or on one product line. Remember, you are after confirmation that the pilot is effective, not yet financial results.
- Limited locations: designed to make pilot more manageable, this type selects one office, a single region, or a sales territory.

The pilot process can range from one worker to an entire office, and the pilot implementation period can be as long as needed. You may want to run the pilot for only a short time—just long enough to work out the bugs in the system, before you move to full implementation—or you might stay in the pilot phase for an extended period of time as you wait for funding or plan for expansion. Once you run a successful pilot, your next step is implementation in the form of a broader rollout.

For the pilot of the IT estimation process described earlier, the team initially built a single "knowledge package," which took approximately one week to compile and provided the background knowledge necessary to offer an accurate estimate for a common but moderately challenging estimate request. This package was assembled using the core team as well as members of the satellite team, who provided the deep knowledge that resided in the heads of experts across the department. The format was repeatedly tested by the team members.

For the pilot, the team trained a mid-level estimator on how to use the knowledge package. When a request for this type of estimate came in, it was redirected to the pilot. The estimator delivered the estimate in less than an hour (down from thirty days) but had many questions as he went; these were answered by members of the team, who observed the pilot from start to finish. The instructions were refined and the results of the pilot were presented to management.

Management then gave the go-ahead to build ten more knowledge packages for a variety of applications. These packages were built, the pilot expanded, and all resulted in a one- to two-hour turnaround time. The team then received approval to build as many knowledge packages as the organization needed for a full rollout and to compile them in a knowledge database.

> ### DID YOU KNOW?
>
> Steve Jobs liked the mouse that Xerox built. But it cost $300 to build and broke within two weeks. Instead, Jobs went to Walgreens and bought all the roll-on underarm deodorant he could find because the applicators had a ball in them. He also bought a butter dish. That was the beginning of the apple-designed mouse.[9]

Launch Phase—Step 2
Implementing Across the Organization

You've done lots of tremendous work up to this juncture, but it can all go off the rails at the point of implementation. Cited as the number-one reason for CEOs failing, final implementation is possibly the hardest part of the entire Q-Loop. Certainly, it's the most important job for senior management, and it's the hardest discipline to achieve throughout an organization. In fact, a significant percent of Fortune 500 CEOs are fired for their inability to execute business strategy.[10] Only through seamless integration of strategy, process, and people, can successful implementation occur.

Given how important implementation efforts are, it's critical to know why 75 percent to 85 percent of them fail.[11] The most widely cited reasons are lack of top management commitment; that management is out of touch with critical events; failure to fully understand the size, scope, and technical aspects of the project; and lack of proper commitment of time and resources. Put all these items together and it's obvious why people become frustrated and burn out, why change initiatives run into endless delays, and, ultimately, why most initiatives fail.

It's an unfortunate series of events. At the beginning of a project, the executive team generally champions an idea—in all likelihood, the idea was generated, refined, or decided on by them. The transition team, generally the next level down from the executive team, may have contributed to the work, and the members likely have exposure to the executive team. As such, they too will probably play a positive role in the implementation. From there, things get a bit murkier.

Opinion leaders are scattered throughout the organization, at all levels. They likely hear about the change through word of mouth, company memos, newsletters, and town hall meetings, and these forums do not inspire belief or passion.

Finally, the workforce, who will likely be tasked with implementing the change and behaving differently, may not have even heard of the change until they're asked to live it. To avoid these many points of disconnect and to increase the likelihood of a successful implementation, involve as many key influencers as possible.

Two Primary Components of Implementation

For a successful implementation, there must be two components: dynamic leadership and an effective plan.

Dynamic Leadership

An active and effective leadership team:

- Sets clear goals and expectations
- Selects the right people to lead the effort and allows them to dedicate themselves fully to achieving the results
- Actively follows through on objectives
- Clears all roadblocks that will inhibit success
- Directly links rewards to performance

Effective Plan

An effective plan asks and answers the following questions:

- What needs to be done?
- Has the plan been thoroughly documented?

- Who will have direct responsibility?
- What other resources are needed to execute the rollout?
- How will relevant employees be trained?
- How will they be evaluated and held accountable?
- What is the timing?
- How will effectiveness be measured?
- How will the effort be communicated?
- Which management processes will need to change to accommodate the redesigned process?

Embrace Resistance

There are many terms that people use for resistance: pushback, lack of buy-in, criticism, foot dragging. None of the terms is positive. People also tend to display resistance in the form of a broad range of unappealing behaviors—from pointed questions to a roll of the eyes to overt sabotage. Generally, I believe that such behaviors are really the perpetrator saying, "You don't know as well as I do." And I tend to agree.

In actuality, resistance is a form of feedback, often provided by people who know more about the day-to-day operations than you do. Dismissing such feedback deprives you of real learning opportunities. When change initiatives run aground, change agents can be quick to point a finger at the people who never got on board. They assume that if only people would stop complaining and offer support, all would be well. Blaming resistors is not only pointless, but can actually lead to destructive managerial behaviors.

To leverage resistance to achieve rapid results, you must understand why the resistance is occurring. Most often, it is because of your organization's norms for solving problems on a day-to-day basis.

I'm not going to spend much more time helping you overcome resistance in your company because, quite honestly, I don't see it in most of my clients. Why? Because that's what the Q-Loop is about—eliminating resistance before it begins.

The effort starts with an idea that comes either from the employee community, the customer, or management. It is ultimately sanctioned by management, who must commit to leading the effort and assigning the company's best and most influential people to the team for thirty days. The Corporate Lab (or some similar experience) then enables people to change their mind-set. This step is critical to opening the minds of the skeptical and showing them what is possible.

From there, we take these former skeptics, who are now excited about change, and give them the freedom, responsibility, and accountability to solve the issue as if they own the company. This ensures they will be leading the implementation charge. The effort only lasts for thirty days, so before management can move on to the "new new thing," and before the team members run out of steam, the team will have a pilot ready, a pilot that is grounded in fact-based analysis and that results from experimentation. The pilot provides the proof to management and to their colleagues that the ideas work. If the rollout involves multiple geographies, additional Labs are used to grease the skids and convert skeptics into promoters.

IDEAS IN ACTION

Recently, I was asked to help a client with an escalating cost issue it was having with its creative production department. Needless to say, resistance to change was palpable. The client prided itself on having outstanding customer service—in fact, the first document visitors saw when they entered the reception area was a framed award the company had received for being voted "Number 1 in Customer Service" in its industry for five consecutive years. As a result, this was a company that never said "no," and the production department was considered one of the jewels within the organization.

So whenever a customer asked for a custom print order, the company complied, without considering cost implications. An even bigger issue was that few in the organization understood the financial impact of their day-to-day decisions.

For example, the company's field sales organization would routinely enter into highly customized one-off deals with clients that cost the company more than it made in revenues. Sales didn't have a clear understanding of the cost and complexity of these transactions. Because they didn't have sufficient information, the sales staff believed that the back-of-the-house design team was sabotaging their deals, while the design groups considered the sales team to be completely out of touch with the realities and constraints of their production environment.

(continued)

This unhealthy dynamic routinely came to a head during end-of-year financial reconciliation, when it became obvious that the division was unprofitable.

Our five-person redesign team included representatives from both sales and design. To address the information asymmetry between front and back of house, the team analyzed two years' worth of client requests and determined that, when viewed individually, they appeared to be unique requests. When viewed in aggregate, however, they did fall into several larger buckets with similar themes. This led the team to develop what they called a "thoughtful customization" approach to the end-to-end design process, which provided clients with the perception of unlimited choice.

The team standardized the end-to-end processes used in more than 90 percent of the requests, and allowed for true customization only in very limited circumstances.

For these customized deals, they established clear back-office processes and analytical support tools to arm salespeople with accurate information on the cost implications of the proposed transactions. They also instituted common reporting standards and tools for both the sales and design teams, to ensure that each group had access to the same data and metrics when making decisions.

The other benefit from the "thoughtful customization" approach was improved turnaround time. Because each project was no longer viewed as a one-off and had standardized pathways to follow, the time to produce "custom" work was reduced from one month to two days.

The solution was incredibly intuitive and, as such, was immediately embraced throughout the organization. By the end of the year, the department was profitable.

Launch Phase—Step 3
Measuring, Monitoring, and Providing Ongoing Feedback

Once the thirty-day initiative is completed, it's essential that you:

- Develop effective documentation to support the new process/strategy/organization
- Select a balanced mix of measures to monitor performance
- Create management reports that convey information quickly and simply

- Develop a plan to take action in case problems arise
- Use the measures…and reward results

But it's not that simple.

Now that the groundbreaking ideas are approved and the team of heroes can finally exhale, you need to embark on the real beginning of the hard work. The beginning, you ask? Yes, the beginning. This is where you translate all the ideas into action.

Far too often, companies believe that the thirty days represents the finish line, when in actuality it's the starting gate. Implementation doesn't happen automatically—it requires the same level of rigor that idea-generation does. I actually find strategy development to be considerably easier than implementation. That's because implementation impacts many individuals and involves emotions, expectations, and real people issues, not just analytics.

I was once brought into a situation by a frantic but perplexed CFO, who said, "I thought we'd done everything right. We designed the strategy by getting input from our people, we communicated it throughout the organization, the board was behind us, and the executive team was aligned. I have no idea how it came off the rails."

Once I got involved, I learned that the strategy itself wasn't the issue. The problem was twofold: lack of effective tactical execution and an inability to effectively govern the program and hold the necessary people accountable. This particular company spent countless hours developing the strategy but little time on the detailed action plan—and would have preferred that someone else sort that mess out.

You see, the trouble is that when it comes to successful implementation, execution tactics are just as critical as strategy. Detailed planning involves breaking work down into smaller parts. In other words:

small = manageable = speed = results = desire to do more = behavioral change = success

I've found that achieving strategic planning and management goals requires an actionable plan that considers the people required to bring the plan to fruition. Sounds simple enough. Yet in practice, both components (plan and people) have challenges and uncertainties that must be carefully managed. An inherent lack of accountability in the planning process leads to problems and sometimes complete failures in execution.

Everyone is accountable for his individual tasks, which are required to achieve the overarching organizational goals; some people, including the CEO, may be accountable for reinforcing the tasks.

Closing a Project

At the end of the thirty days, the project will likely be completed. In my experience, several members of the team may be reluctant to end their work. They may find their work on the team to be more fulfilling than their regular job, they may miss the camaraderie of the team, or they may miss the attention within the organization that working on the team provided. As difficult as it may be for the team to end its work, the project does have an end and, given how hard the team worked over the thirty-day period, it's imperative that team members return to their original jobs once the mandate has been achieved.

It's also important that every project has formal closure. This is an occasion to recognize the considerable time and effort that went into the initiative. It's also an opportunity to capture what was learned from the project and share it with the team sponsor. Closure can signal that the responsibility for the standardization, monitoring, and often the implementation can now shift to others in the organization.

The following elements are part of an effective project closure:

Evaluating the team's work: Although the project is ending, it is likely that the team members will be involved with future efforts. Taking the time to do a final evaluation of the project reinforces key lessons and provides a sense of completion for the team. The evaluation often includes a list of key lessons learned, a review of the team's strengths and achievements, and a review of individual team members' development objectives for improvement. In addition, the evaluation should include a discussion of improvements that the organization can make to increase the efficiency and effectiveness of future projects, along with recommendations for where the team's recommendations could be replicated elsewhere in the organization.

Completing the documentation: The team's documentation serves as the organization's memory of the team's work. It is therefore important to finish writing up the results, key insights, and critical next steps (including a detailed implementation plan).

Sharing the results: There are many ways teams can share their results with the rest of the organization—once the team has been given clearance to do so by the project champion. The team can give a presentation, write an article for the company newsletter, post a storyboard, or send a company-wide e-mail.

Celebrate the success: It's important to celebrate success with not only the team members, but with everyone who supported the effort. You may wish to include people who covered for the team members so they could work on the project; those who helped with the surveys, data collection,

RESISTANT INDUSTRIES OPERATING PRINCIPLE #41
"Your responsibility is to make sure your boss is happy with your work. If everybody can do that, the customers will be happy as well."

and analysis; and, of course, the project champion. A team lunch, dinner, or other special event is a positive way to provide powerful closure to the project.

Snorkeling Versus Deep Sea Diving

In the hope that it offers you some inspiration, I'd like to share a final brief account of just how powerful a small team of invested employees can be. One of my clients had been living for many years with a set of homegrown systems that were cobbled together and less than efficient. Against my recommendation, the company decided to purchase a holistic, fully integrated system from an expert provider with deep experience in this field. The system provider sent three of its consultants to live with the client for three weeks to fully understand the nature of their business, their system requirements, and the issues they were facing.

After the three weeks, the consultants delivered a report that restated the high-level view of the issues that senior management already possessed. IT issues were the central theme, and the consultant was unable to articulate how the new system would optimize the customer experience.

At that point, the senior manager recognized that the expert provider's solution was not adequate, and we tried a different approach. Using The Corporate Lab and then pursuing a mandate that would meet the senior manager's requirements, we created a solution with a cross-functional, six-person team that worked four hours a day for two days. At the end of the session, the team had built an enterprise map from the perspective of the customer and laid the system work flow over the processes. All system issues were identified, pain points were clearly articulated, manual interventions were documented, and rework was calculated. In the words of the client, "The consultant went snorkeling and you went deep sea diving." Our insights were richer, the focus was clearer, and what the organization required to move forward became apparent.

Certainly, the initial consulting effort was poor. However, three clear messages emerged. The volume of work that can be generated by a highly focused, cross-functional team of internal experts is tremendous. The buy-in for self-generated work is far higher than it is for work produced by an outside agency. And the ability of an outside voice to ask all the right questions—and the willingness of a client to share all of its issues—is sometimes in question.

CHAPTER 6 TAKEAWAY

Be sure to have all of the preliminary steps (explained in chapter 4) completed before putting the information in this chapter into practice.

Coming into the meeting that will launch your thirty-day project to achieve your mandate, team members will be excited, anxious, possibly fatigued, and likely a bit confused. Remind team members why they were selected for the team, that they will receive support from management, and what the mandate is.

Be sure that every team member understands that there is only one customer: the person who pays the bill.

The Results Triangle will help you systematically and consistently deliver on the promises you make to your customer.

Companies that adapt a test-and-learn approach by using rapid experimentation will deliver fact-based results in a fraction of the time it takes using traditional problem-solving techniques.

COMING UP

Maintaining the energy and commitment inspired over the thirty-day project period is difficult, and there's still a risk that your organization will revert to its old patterns. The next chapter offers insight into how senior management and leaders throughout your organization can ensure that you keep the positive momentum going.

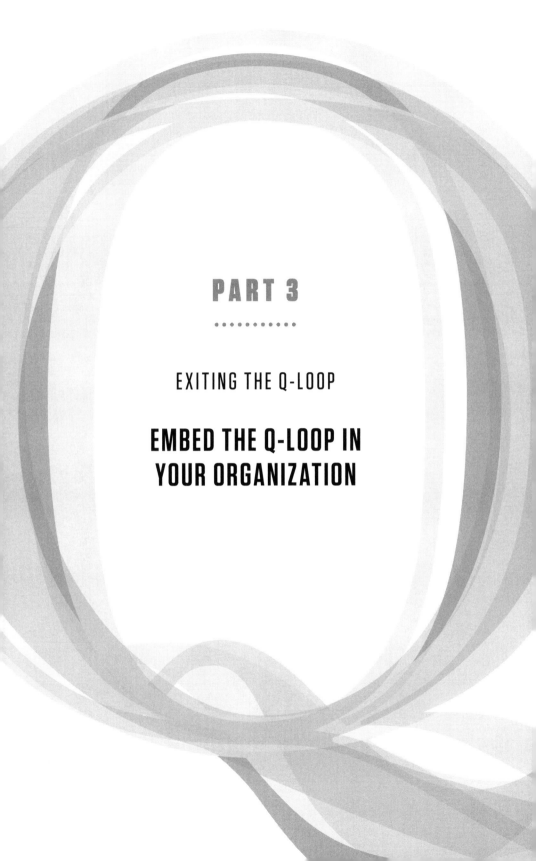

PART 3

· · · · · · · · · · ·

EXITING THE Q-LOOP

EMBED THE Q-LOOP IN YOUR ORGANIZATION

7

Ignite a Wildfire of Pull

A life spent making mistakes is not only more honorable but more useful than a life spent doing nothing.
—GEORGE BERNARD SHAW

Energy and persistence conquer all things.
—BENJAMIN FRANKLIN

It's been about thirty short days since you assembled your team of heroes, identified your mandate, and completed a pilot program to prove the concept, and the change initiative is now being unleashed within your organization. It's a fantastic accomplishment—and in some ways the hardest part of the Q-Loop is behind you. With the tools you now have, this project should have run more smoothly and been more ambitious, been more successful, and been completed far faster than any previous major change effort you have attempted.

Now the questions are: How can you be sure not only that this change initiative takes root but that future initiatives run smoothly as well? And even more importantly, how can you make certain that the energy you triggered over the past month gets embedded into your organization's DNA? How can you make sure that every single worker acts and fundamentally feels like an empowered owner with an important stake in the organization's future (and not just her small slice of it)?

My intention for this book continues to be helping you uncover and capture bold new ideas, unlock your untapped potential, profit from your

— **DID YOU KNOW?** —

You can tell me about a change effort that resulted from reading this book or share your insights with me at bklapper@theklapperinstitute.com.

collective organizational IQ, and identify and empower team after team of heroes. But as the subtitle bluntly declares, the overarching goal is to help you produce *lasting* change. To do so, you must achieve an ever-increasing array of powerful mandates so that your organization thrives and evolves long into the future.

It's a mighty ambition—and one that can be accomplished only with your continued work.

Here is where the executive management team needs to take ownership of the process and be the true leaders they were charged with being. Too often, organizations set the strategic direction for the change and then the leaders remain remote, leaving the actual change to less motivated people. It's a cause for defeat. Add to it lack of senior management commitment, projects taking too long to demonstrate tangible results, lack of engagement by the people responsible for the implementation, an overriding assumption that an integrated (albeit complex) information technology solution is the answer to fundamental operational deficiencies, or the belief that "we've tried everything and nothing has worked for this company"—and you have the sure recipe for failure.

It's time to eradicate all of these detrimental attitudes and actions and replace them with the following four key strategies to ignite a wildfire throughout your organization for all future change initiatives. A bit later in the chapter, I'll give you more detail about each strategy.

First, the most successful transformations occur when executives create and sustain real energy within their organizations. Sounds simple, but it's not.

Second, executives must communicate objectives clearly, compellingly, and repeatedly.

Third, executives must raise employees' expectations, actively change people's behavior, and engage everyone at all levels throughout the organization.

And fourth, transformation is a coordinated, ongoing effort—not a program with a defined beginning, middle, and end. My experience tells me that there's a big misunderstanding about what true transformation is. But not in this book. And I hope not in your future.

IDEAS IN ACTION

A major insurance company I recently worked with faced a substantial challenge. It needed to standardize its underwriting process across eight underwriting centers, each with a different organizational structure. As it was, each location used a different process; had different job titles, roles, and levels of authority; and held a conviction that its way was optimal.

Management recognized that to create scale in operations, for growth and to reduce costs, they needed to balance caseloads across the system—which could only be accomplished by standardization. For years, the company had recognized the need for this work and had tried with fits and starts, but the changes couldn't get real traction. Employees simply didn't buy into the concept.

To break down paradigms and expand employees' views of what was possible, we ran The Corporate Lab with a team made up of two representatives from each of the locations. After the Lab, we kicked off the project by telling the team that we were going to create a new company that would put their existing underwriting operation out of business. We asked each team member to contribute $50 to start the new organization. Our purpose was to create the emotional engagement needed to overcome the tremendous initial skepticism.

To establish a consistent flow of work (one of the company's objectives), we changed from a "push" to a "pull" system. In a push system, each underwriter is allocated a certain number of cases a day. In a push system, cases are sent to underwriters regardless of whether they are ready to take on new ones. Some underwriters finished as early as noon, when they hit their daily quota. But when underwriters were dealing with complicated cases, they weren't always able to get to all of the cases in their queue, so there would be unresolved cases at the end of a shift. There was no way for cases to get "pushed" back into the system, so they went to a special "overflow" handling area and their pricing was delayed. If the department switched to a pull system, on the other hand, underwriters could grab a case when they were free. The result? Cases would get underwritten more quickly.

To overcome resistance, we piloted both the shift in responsibilities and the pull system in one of the underwriting offices for a week. Representatives from the team flew to the pilot location to train the local underwriters on the new process and outline their new

(continued)

responsibilities. Both new elements were immediately embraced by the participants and, within four weeks, the pilot was expanded to the other locations, which immediately reported similar findings.

Neither change cost anything to implement and there was no need for a new underwriting system. It had the added benefit of giving people a sense of control over their own work, measurably boosting department morale. The company was still able to manage how much work people did, but took a different approach to managing it—measuring the number of cases each underwriter completed each month.

This idea, in fact, saved millions of dollars by turning the company's staffing pyramid upside down. Instead of using dozens of experienced senior underwriters, the company really needed more junior underwriters who could handle a regular stream of simpler cases; senior underwriters could then be used exclusively for the more difficult cases.

Future Change Initiatives Survey

Please respond to the following statements by circling the number that best describes your opinion.

1 = Strongly disagree
2 = Disagree
3 = Neutral opinion
4 = Agree
5 = Strongly agree

When considering a change mandate, the organization always comes first and the way the change impacts individuals comes second.

1   2   3   4   5

If I think something must be changed, I spend a long time planning it before kicking off a change project.

1   2   3   4   5

I rarely talk with frontline employees and team members about what is causing the need for change.

1   2   3   4   5

Even if I don't have senior management's full support, I proceed with change initiatives because a good idea is worth it.

| 1 | 2 | 3 | 4 | 5 |

I create a change plan for my team and department and let other departments deal with the effects.

| 1 | 2 | 3 | 4 | 5 |

I communicate success within my department but not throughout the organization.

| 1 | 2 | 3 | 4 | 5 |

I believe that if the change makes financial and operational sense, then it will work.

| 1 | 2 | 3 | 4 | 5 |

When working on a change project, I expect team members to perform double duty.

| 1 | 2 | 3 | 4 | 5 |

After implementing a change project, everyone deserves a substantial break before moving on to the next project.

| 1 | 2 | 3 | 4 | 5 |

My organization has managed change initiatives badly in the past, so future change projects will be problematic.

| 1 | 2 | 3 | 4 | 5 |

Results Key

Add the results of the survey and compare the total to the following.

40–50 = You are well positioned to succeed at future change initiatives. You have a strong understanding of what makes change successful and you have a good knowledge of managing, planning, and implementing change. You seem to grasp the concepts in this chapter (and the previous chapters of the book).

30-39 = You are fairly well positioned to succeed at future change initiatives. You understand many of the elements required for change, and putting them into practice usually works, although you sometimes run into obstacles. Review this chapter (and the previous chapters of the book) to improve your ability to create and sustain change.

20-29 = You will struggle with future change initiatives. You tend to look only at results and don't focus enough on how to achieve these results. To improve your chances of success with change, you must do a better job of communicating and sharing successes throughout your organization to create the necessary support. Study this chapter (and review the previous three chapters) to improve your ability to create and sustain change.

10-19 = You are poorly positioned to succeed at future change initiatives. You look at end results and don't focus on how to achieve these results. To be successful with change, you must communicate and share the excitement throughout your organization to create the necessary support. Study this chapter (and review the previous three chapters) to improve your ability to create and sustain change.

IDEAS IN ACTION

Several years ago, I was having dinner with the president and chief operating officer of one of the world's largest beauty products company. She asked me, "Brian, do you think sales is an art or a science?"

I replied, "Sales is most certainly a science, but it's best performed by artists." By that, I meant that an effective sales process can and should be documented, repeated, and measured, yet not everybody can excel in a well-designed sales process, as many other personal traits are required.

She agreed, and then went on to explain an issue she was having at her company. It involved a document that the company had created several years earlier. It was well designed and thoughtfully prepared, describing in detail the sales process that the company wanted to use globally. The issue was that, although management believed the guidelines were intuitive, no country was using them.

As a result, every country was using its own sales process, which delivered mixed results and made it nearly impossible to evaluate performance on a global basis. The CEO asked me, "Can you help us design and implement a best-practice sales process that will be embraced by our five million independent representatives in over one hundred countries?"

"Is that all?" I laughed, but I was genuinely impressed by the request.

The first thing we did was transform the CEO's question into a formal mandate: "Perform a global diagnostic to determine the company's best-practice sales process and create a single sales process that representatives will want to implement globally. Once implemented, the new global process will improve field fundamentals and sales productivity, deliver a consistent sales approach, and enable management to measure and compare sales performance on a country-by-country basis." The mandate was approved by the executive management team and they designated one of their most respected senior managers to lead the effort.

Next, we identified a transglobal team of eight high-potential employees from North America, South America, Europe, and Asia, all fully dedicated to the project for six weeks. We put all the team members through The Corporate Lab to launch the initiative. Immediately following the Lab, each team member visited two countries that were not in his region and spent three days in the field with representatives observing the sales process.

When the team returned from the field, they shared two stunning revelations. First, the greatest difference in the sales process across the sixteen countries they had visited wasn't process, but language. Second, there wasn't a single country that was performing the end-to-end process at best-practice levels. When the team presented their observations to the executive team, the executives were equally surprised.

The team then documented its observations and formulated the new global sales process as four primary steps: Prospect, Appoint, Train, Develop (PATD). All countries were performing all four of these steps, albeit with different levels of rigor, measurement, and incentive systems and, therefore, different levels of success. Once the macro process was developed, the global team broke each of the primary steps into five best-practice sub-steps, resulting in a twenty-step global process.

When the team compared its new process with what they'd observed in the field, they calculated that at least fifteen of the twenty sub-steps were being performed—but with different levels

(continued)

of effectiveness. For each sub-step, the global team defined inputs and outputs, roles and responsibilities, key evaluation measures, and guidance for collateral.

The executive leadership team agreed that if each of the countries would implement the twenty-step sub-process, the team would fully achieve its mandate. The most interesting aspect of this project is what happened next: getting the different countries, with their very different cultures, to buy into (and fully implement) the new global process.

We started with a pilot that began in three countries: Mexico, Germany, and the Philippines. Because everyone realized that sales is not a twenty-step process but a hundred-step process, we encouraged each of the three pilot countries to develop a localized hundred-step sales process that ultimately rolled up into the global twenty-step process. We ran The Corporate Lab in each of the three countries and formed a team of five participants for each pilot country. The mandate for each of the teams was "to 'localize' the twenty-step global sales process by developing a detailed set of country-specific procedures that would provide the detail needed to implement the global sales process." Each team worked full-time for one month to create the local procedure manual.

Once the three manuals were created, the new procedures were launched in specific regions within each of the three countries. The team was responsible for ensuring compliance with the new procedures, coaching the field, noting where the procedures needed to be improved, and collecting the performance measures. After several months, the new process was expanded to other regions, and finally to the entire country.

As the pilot countries implemented the new process, we ran Corporate Labs throughout the world to allow additional countries to localize the global process. Labs were run in Argentina, Brazil, Chile, Venezuela, Great Britain, Hungary, Italy, Japan, and Taiwan. Eventually, other countries were included, and the new sales process was implemented globally.

Create and Sustain Real Energy

At many organizations I've worked with, projects that begin with The Corporate Lab and then run along the thirty-day time frame described in the last chapter become known as Klapper projects. I couldn't be prouder that my name is associated with an undertaking that's powered by such impressive work and such a wonderful spirit of camaraderie.

I'm also delighted that they are successful. At the risk of sounding immodest, I have never worked with a company on a thirty-day mandate that hasn't been successful. And the success is not because of me. What is normally incredibly difficult can really be so intuitively simple: assemble the right people, dedicate some of their time, provide them with a crisp objective, and get them to embrace the possibility that there might be a better way. (Okay, this last part is hard.)

As soon as possible, revisit chapters 4, 5, and 6 and create a new team and a new mandate; use the same mind-set–shifting exercises and perspectives to inspire another team of heroes composed of more top-performing, influential employees. Use members of the previous team as advocates to promote the experience. Use management to demonstrate that they see members of such teams as more valuable than ever. Establish more wins and run them up the flagpole by putting them in your newsletter, describing them at a town hall meeting, or posting them on an internal blog (or even an external one if it makes sense).

Begin to set clearly defined and well-communicated goals for the next thirty-six months. Then build a project portfolio that demonstrates success with a combination of project types, ranging from bigger, longer-term strategy projects, to money projects that result in good ROI, to customer-facing projects that thrill your customers—all of them with the same thirty-day time frame.

All together, nothing could be better for energizing others and encouraging them to get involved with a Klapper project. A principal reason that so many change programs collapse is that management fails to move from talking to action quickly enough. This leads to mixed messages and gives resistance a better opportunity to set in. You're at a critical juncture, just at the threshold of overcoming resistance. It's not the time to hem and haw. Don't let bureaucracy kill momentum with endless reviews, unnecessary meetings, and ongoing debates.

After some minor flare-ups of resistance, because such projects can be perceived as a distraction from day-to-day responsibilities, people will see the swift and resounding successes. Word will spread quickly (as you help to spread it in every way possible) and the shared attitude will quickly make a 180-degree turn. Soon, people will clamber to get on a Klapper project. With the additional successes of these new projects, resistance will be converted into passion.

Velocity helps too. Be sure all projects focus on achieving rapid results and not on some elaborate process. Client after client has shown me process maps and presentation decks from process improvement initiatives that took more than nine months to create—and were never fully implemented. There were often excellent ideas buried within the work, but the project simply took too long, management support waned, and organizational momentum died.

Likewise, don't forget the lessons learned in chapter 5 regarding The Corporate Lab—learning to re-see the way you operate every day. Or chapter 6—coming to see that there is a better method to accomplish change. It's essential that you link learning with doing and that each new team has an opportunity to experience the same sort of shift in perspective. For me, learning is the Lab. I never run a project without a Lab. It breaks down resistance and teaches the tools. So remember that it is the last two chapters that enable people to learn the art of the possible. Without these experiences, you are setting a project up for pitfalls. At numerous organizations, I run hundreds of Labs to change the mind-set of twenty people at a time. While you may not have this option, use the methodologies I outlined earlier to do something similar.

As you develop and pursue mandates, focus on both quantitative performance (including more stringent operational and financial metrics) and corporate health (including the softer metrics of sustainability and continuous improvement, which help to take the temperature of the organization). And as you build your teams, identify key influencers at all levels of your organization and bring them on board for specific initiatives, which will go a long way toward creating a culture of enthusiastic employees.

Returning to the concept I discussed in chapter 3, make sure the front line feels ownership and empowerment for change. Senior management needs to proactively address the negative emotions—anxiety, confusion, frustration, anger, and exhaustion—that can kick in among employees and stifle an otherwise achievable initiative. Keeping the projects moving quickly—thirty days, ideally—prevents this negativity from kicking in.

Speaking of exhaustion, day thirty-one of a project is when it usually creeps in, which is another reason that sixty-day or ninety-day or six-month projects often fail. Projects completed in thirty days, on the other hand, are swift enough to sustain collective verve throughout. It's striking how often I've been told by Klapper project team members that they never worked so hard, thought so much, or had as much fun as they did on a

Klapper team. It's because they felt empowered and were rewarded with success before other negative facets emerged.

Think about it this way: when employees feel hampered, little but negativity arises. Do you remember the Toyota recalls that began in 2009? During the recall crisis, Toyota didn't change its management style one bit, continuing to tightly control every decision. When American managers found defects in vehicles, they had to follow a tortuous bureaucratic process and were often met with skepticism and defensiveness by the Japanese office.

> **DID YOU KNOW?**
>
> A cornerstone of its expansion strategy, McDonald's adapts its menu around the world to meet local tastes. International menu items include McSpicy Paneer in India, Bacon Potato Pie in Japan, Shae Shake Fries with Seaweed in China, McKebab in Israel, McPinto in Costa Rica, Rosti Brekki Wrap in Australia, and, of course, McBeer in Germany.[1]

Compare this to Toyota's response during the tsunami catastrophe of 2011. Damaged plants disrupted the supply of more than five hundred parts. To fix this pressing issue, the CEO assembled general managers of departments and took the unprecedented step of instructing them to restore production and not waste time reporting upward. Within two months, all but thirty of five hundred parts were available.[2] Why did they wait for a crisis to empower the managers?

Communicate Goals and Successes Compellingly

In addition to the obvious benefit of your initial mandate's success, another huge benefit is that you now have a wonderful opportunity to broadcast this early success loudly, proudly, and often. And not for the sake of boasting. In fact, sharing triumphs is an essential strategy that positions your organization for future successes. You've not only proved the concept of the mandate, you have also proved the concept of the approach. Everyone needs to know it. By demonstrating success, you encourage other areas of your organization to quickly embrace the approach and outlook—especially if it is clear to those employees that the ideas of their peers were recognized and implemented.

While the iron is hot, do everything you can to help the organization roll out the pilot and then quickly commence another high-profile project—or several simultaneously. It's important to make sure that people in the organization experience some early wins, which will increase individual support for change while also helping to sway the attitudes of change-skeptical employees. As you're working on thirty-day pilot programs, celebrate and recognize progress along the way—by sharing success stories, promoting a collective future vision, and sustaining a continued commitment to transformation.

Share as much information with colleagues as is appropriate during a project. How much to share depends on the mandate. If the mandate is to increase wallet share, it won't frighten employees, so it's valuable to share. If the mandate is to remove $10 million in costs from the system, then people will be made anxious by the change, so information about the project shouldn't be leaked. You want input from the organization, but there should also be ground rules regarding confidentiality.

Communicate the positive stuff in a tweet, a blog, or by e-mail. For example, "We talked to customers today. Interesting stuff!" Or "Big learning today on the Klapper team! Can't wait to share!" Agree among the team what can and cannot be said. In the final analysis, there are times when it makes sense for team members to talk with their fellow employees to spread the word and times when it doesn't make sense. There are also times when you'll simply move too fast for substantive updates with anyone but the project champion and some key stakeholders.

Team members can serve as ambassadors. For example, if there seems to be stress in the organization regarding the change that's going on behind the curtain, ambassadors can report back (maybe people worry that organizational changes are going to occur, for example). As a result, it might be decided that it's time for a town hall meeting among a particular group to lower the temperature.

Next, make sure senior managers live the change they want to see throughout the organization. Articulating a clear vision of the change you want to accomplish will help everyone understand what you're asking them to do and, more important, why. Create an easy-to-understand elevator pitch (you know, a brief explanation of the change that can be told in the time it takes you to travel a few floors in the elevator), and connect it to everything you do. Include in your vision current issues that need to be overcome and offer an inspiring view of your organization's future state. Make it emotional.

Don't just share your vision once and expect people to get it. They won't. Most successful transformations reinforce core messages through regular, timely communications that are both practical and inspirational. Communicate the heck out of it and tie your vision for the change to every part of the organization's operation that you can, including training, new hires, and performance reviews.

Don't overlook your audience's point of view as you create this story. Employees want to know what's in it for them. How will it make their life easier? What is the benefit? Because the collective culture of an organization is an aggregate of what is common to all of its individual mind-sets, a transformation can entail changing the minds of hundreds or thousands of individuals. Don't forget about these individuals as you consider the larger organization.

Again, the fact that these projects move swiftly helps people digest the big changes that are afoot. They don't have to live under a cloud of uncertainly for nine months. In thirty days, they'll know the story. At the very least, it can be communicated that the results of the project will be unveiled in thirty days, which will help reduce anxiety.

> **DID YOU KNOW?**
>
> The fear of change is called tropophobia. The "tropo" part of the word literally means to turn or to bend.

Finally, it's important to communicate how employees' work will change and how they will be measured during and after the change effort. Setting clear expectations and providing frequent informal feedback will help build employee confidence and shape the key behaviors needed for positive results.

Raise Employees' Expectation

Individuals in organizations, to embrace change, must also engage in a process that reshapes how they think about themselves, not just about their jobs. For this to occur, change needs to become part of your organization's culture. Accordingly, the surrounding structures—reward and recognition systems, for example—must be in tune with these new behaviors (see page 39 regarding intrinsic versus extrinsic motivation). Employees must be given the skills and support to do what's required of them. And they must see people they respect modeling it every day. Together, these conditions add up to a way of fundamentally changing employee behaviors and attitudes.

Keep in mind that change can be unsettling for everyone in your organization. After all, think about what it can mean for long-term employees who have been there for, say, ten or twenty years. They need to know how change will affect them and what the future state of the organization will look and feel like. If employees believe in the organization's overall purpose, and this purpose is in alignment with their own purpose, they will be far more inclined to change their individual behaviors. In the end, employees will alter their mind-set only if they see the point of the change and agree with it, at least enough to give it a try. Then, with success, they'll be willing to try again.

Employees must also understand the role of their actions and how it relates to the company's overarching success. And employees must believe that they play a part and understand what that part is. It's not enough to merely tell them that they'll have to do things differently. You need to communicate a compelling story: *Why is this undertaking important? Why are the contributions of each employee essential? Where are we going?*

Despite the importance of the senior management team leading the change, it's not just about the few influence leaders talking the talk—it's about generating a groundswell of support for the change. If you have a mass of employees behind the need for ongoing change, your battle is half over. As mentioned before, generating energy and proclaiming your victories will help to energize people. Another powerful way is finding the most talented people and bringing them into the effort.

This strategy was largely explained in chapter 4 as part of creating a team of heroes, but think about it again in this slightly different context. Your heroes won't just help you achieve your mandates; they'll also help to influence coworkers who aren't as easily swayed by senior management. Sometimes leaders can tell the most compelling, meaningful story possible and some employees will resist it nonetheless. Whether it's their inclination to rebel against authority or to close their minds to higher-ups, it's a common occurrence. But enlisting the most influential frontline workers will go a long way toward changing the hearts and minds of a critical mass.

If you have a problem that needs to be solved, who are the best people to help you solve it? It's the people living and breathing the problem—not some branch manager who understands just some of the aspects of the issue. You need people who are respected by their peers. And you need to put them on teams that represent all of the issues in play. Organizations that do not leverage the knowledge and passion of their frontline heroes often find themselves incapable of effecting significant change.

For change to be successful, *all* key influencers must model the way. When that occurs, a larger message can be conveyed: *We expect more from*

you. We expect more from ourselves. We expect better from this organiza-
tion than what we've delivered in the past.

To further this message, you also need to establish true accountability within your organization. As difficult as it can be, a public hanging is sometimes needed to make your commitment known. If you're going to ask team after team of heroes to do this hard work, and word gets out that management tolerates mediocrity or doesn't implement what the team comes up with because of resistance that could have been avoided, it puts the whole undertaking at risk. If a manager doesn't buy into it, maybe it's not because the idea and plan weren't great ones. Maybe it's because the idea wasn't his, or maybe he was previously responsible for solving the problem and didn't come up with a viable solution himself. Maybe he doesn't trust the people below him, or maybe the solution is counterintuitive to what he believes, or maybe he's just a change-resistant guy, or maybe the team came up with a solution that minimizes this resistor as the hero, or . . .

You get the idea. I hope you also get the idea that such a person might need to be let go from your organization to promote a greater good.

In short, employees resist change for lots of reasons. They might simply disagree with the change or the rationale it's based on. Or they might believe the change will be a fad. Or there might be deeper psychological factors, such as a fear of learning new skills, loss of authority, concern over their roles becoming redundant, increased hours, or a number of other possibilities. When these feelings emerge, the result can be employees who feel helpless, angry, frustrated, or complacent, and as a result become resistant to change. It's your job to address it before it happens.

Ensure That Transformation Is an Ongoing Effort

There's a common misconception of what real transformation is. Okay, so you want to take 20 percent of costs out of an operating budget. That's a valuable pursuit. But it isn't the end-all of a transformation. Transformation isn't an initiative, like a process reengineering project. Transformation is a perpetual process, and it involves all members of your organization.

It's imperative that you don't view your transformation as a "change program." Change programs so often fail because they are seen as just—*programs.* A mentality of "Now we're going to make changes and then we'll get back to normal" causes the failure. Change, as the saying goes, is a constant. So a one-off program, which presumably has a start and a finish, doesn't address the need for the long-term change required throughout the organization.

You need to continuously create new organizational capabilities. You need to break down silos. You need to build a new incentive system consistent with transformation objectives to reinforce and embed change.

Nah, it's been going well for me. I think I'll stay like this.

The transformation effort must also be custom designed to fit your unique organizational requirements. This means that the people responsible for implementing the process transformation must be engaged in its development. Think about it: a highly efficient, virtual organization lies buried beneath your company's infrastructure. It doesn't have an organization chart or defined reporting relationships. But these many unrecognized heroes, working underground in this virtual organization, are the ones directly responsible for actually getting things done. It's also these heroes, often acting independently, who have historically been the largest obstacles to achieving any kind of process transformation. This dynamic makes it nearly impossible for an outside agency to fully understand how this unseen organization operates and how to craft a solution that will be embraced by it. That's why it's up to you.

In addition, off-the-shelf solutions rarely work for transformation. Instead, you need to rely on the knowledge, culture, politics, and operating rules specific to your organization to craft a unique solution that will work within your complex, distinctive operating environment. The only constant from one organization to another is the key ingredient: people. A successful change program, therefore, must focus on what people think and believe. This powerful knowledge must then be translated to generate solutions that are pulled across the enterprise and down through the organization's many layers.

Transformation involves fundamental changes to your organization's strategy, organizational structure, operating systems, capabilities, and culture. And all of these elements need to be right and aligned. Leaders aren't always prepared for the change of management style required to manage a changed business or one where change is the norm.

Needless to say, but I'll say it anyway: it's hard. And it's why so many change programs don't work. But addressing these pitfalls is precisely what will keep you from being tripped up by them.

How Brands Adapt

In 1850, Buffalo, NY, American Express was an express mail business.

Nintendo started by making handmade playing cards.

Samsung's origins have more to do with fruits, veggies, dried fish, and noodles than consumer electronics.

Shell began as a company that sold ... shells. As in sea shells.

Create a Dedicated Transformation Office

Change within an organization affects every part of it, from the bottom to the top. Yet too often these functional areas operate as silos, without cohesive communication of the key objectives that impact their operation and the larger organization. The best change management solves this dilemma by creating a dedicated Transformation Office that has sustained executive support.

How does such an office help? By enabling your organization to implement, monitor and reward, communicate, and report on change. An effective Transformation Office also involves stakeholders from each functional area with clearly defined roles and responsibilities that align with the objectives of each group and the organization as a whole.

If you don't feel it's important enough to have a Transformation Office to prioritize among the hundreds of possible projects, then you won't demonstrate to the organization that you want real transformation. I'll go so far as to say that failure to create a dedicated Transformation Office means you don't value change enough to nurture it.

Potential members of a Transformation Office need to understand the explicit benefits and career opportunities that will be open to them as a result of joining the change effort. The best employees often hesitate to take an assignment that may, in some cases, last only eighteen to thirty-six months—which is usually the minimum amount of time required for a transformation—fearing that it will damage their careers in the long run.

To counter these fears, it's beneficial to develop a formal career plan for change agents. Consider making participation a requirement for promotion to senior management. Or build a career-development track within the program. Such strategies can be effective recruiting tools, motivating candidates by offering benefits—including opportunities to build new skills, exposing them to new areas of knowledge, and offering a path to career advancement.

Not long ago, a senior executive asked me the following question: "Brian, how can I get people to sidetrack their current career path and buy into becoming part of a Transformation Office?" His concern was that it sounded a bit temporary. True, I said. There's a chance that after three years, because you've only created a thirty-six-month time line, things could change (then again, perhaps not). To allay his fear, I asked him to imagine himself in his thirties again. Then I asked him to imagine his younger self being offered the opportunity to solve the organization's and chairman's and executive committee's and board's most pressing problems as his full-time job. I added, "How would *that* have looked on your resume?"

He was convinced.

Primary Responsibilities of a Transformation Office

Implement change. A Transformation Office implements thoughtful processes, procedures, and tools (including budgeting and financial control, change control, quality oversight, planning, risk and issue management, resource management, and more). A Transformation Office must have established, consistent, repeatable project management practices and tools that are in use across the organization. All projects need to be held to the same standards and requirements for success. A Transformation Office must also establish clear and specific management responsibility, accountability, and control over business transformation–related activities and applicable resources.

RESISTANT INDUSTRIES OPERATING PRINCIPLE #3
"Culture can't be seen and it can't be measured—therefore
it cannot be changed. We are who we are."

Monitor and reward change. A Transformation Office must have visibility into the progress and cost of all projects. Members must know exactly how resources are being used across projects so they can distribute this cost, schedule, and resource information to the appropriate stakeholders throughout the organization. This office must have the power to measure performance and grant rewards that are consistent with the behaviors people are asked to embrace. When the organization's goals of promoting new attitudes and behaviors aren't reinforced, employees are far more likely to resist change. For example, if managers are asked to spend time coaching junior employees but coaching doesn't figure into their performance scorecards, they're less likely to do it or do it well. As a result, the Transformation Office must develop a clear strategic and integrated plan for business transformation with specific goals, measures, and accountability mechanisms to monitor progress.

Communicate change. Members of the Transformation Office should facilitate communities of practice to promote project management best practices within their organizations. These communities of practice provide project managers with a forum so they can share their insights and learn from each other's experiences to solve project management issues. The Transformation Office must also continually solicit key stakeholders to find out the idea-generating opportunities that are important to them.

Report on change. The Transformation Office must have a leader who reports to C-level executives. The leader must be granted authority to enforce changes, as well as accountability for supporting practices that promote success. This office must focus on the critical metrics—both at a project level and at an organizational level. In addition to metrics associated with cost and schedule, the Transformation Office must track criteria important to the organization, such as customer satisfaction and process improvement.

Job description for Transformation Office leader. The Transformation Office leader directs business transformation projects at the global, corporate level. She takes accountability and responsibility for management of all aspects of global, corporate programs. The leader drives changes in the business that lead to adoption of new practices; designs and executes workshops that drive diverse, cross-functional groups to agreement on lean, repeatable processes. In addition, she is responsible for a wide range of decisions regarding transformation implementation, strategic business priorities, client impacting strategies, budget, resource management and allocation, and issue resolution.

CHAPTER 7 TAKEAWAY

It's time to achieve an ever-increasing array of powerful mandates so that your organization thrives and evolves long into the future.

Executive leadership needs to create and sustain real energy.

Leadership must communicate goals and successes compellingly.

Leadership must raise employee expectations.

And executive leadership must ensure that transformation is an ongoing effort.

One of the primary methods of proving that transformation is an ongoing effort is by creating a dedicated Transformation Office.

COMING UP

Read about the Q-Loop in action as an organization embraces it to achieve organization-wide change.

8

A Story of Change

Art is not what you see, but what you make others see.
—EDGAR DEGAS

Intuition will tell the thinking mind where to look next.
—JONAS SALK

When I was a kid, I loved hearing stories. In school, at home, wherever. I always felt like I learned so much from them, sometimes even more than I learned from lessons in school, which seemed a bit abstract. A story, on the other hand, always felt so pertinent, like it could show me how to handle a situation. To this day, I feel the same way. I'm all for solid information, facts, and meaningful lessons. But a story brings facts and information to life. In that spirit, let me ask you: How about a story?

In my humble opinion, I have a great one to share with you, which shows you the Q-Loop in its entirety. Of the many organizations I have worked with over the years, from Fortune 100 financial services firms to global consumer products companies to multibillion-dollar energy companies—any of which would make a compelling story to illustrate the Q-Loop in action—there is an especially complex one that I keep coming back to.

In my professional career, it was the one that most challenged me, pushed me the hardest, inspired me, and absolutely delighted the customer. There are perhaps others that could impress you even more, but that's not my biggest wish right now. What I want more than anything is to inspire you and illuminate the process as much as I possibly can in this final chapter. And so I've chosen the following story to illustrate an organization taking the journey around the Q-Loop and poising itself for greatness. The bumps along the way only make the story more interesting.

Priszm Brands Faces a Challenge

In 2007, one of the biggest operators of quick-service restaurants in Canada—which ran chains including KFC, Taco Bell, and Pizza Hut—was experiencing some difficulties. Priszm's stock price had dropped from $13.50 to $1.50. Its previous thirteen monthly promotions hadn't generated the expected or desired results. Add to that the fact that same-store sales growth and traffic were in decline, profits were being impacted by inflationary challenges, and the restaurants' customer base was eroding. The KFC brand, in particular, wasn't resonating with customers. And making any sort of implementation of change initiatives was next to impossible because field employee turnover exceeded a staggering 200 percent. It added up to a less than ideal picture.

Among the struggles faced by the organization was that every activity and process existed within a functional department, with no forum to bring together ideas that could benefit the entire organization. Many employees who were in the trenches day to day were aware of individual problems, but there was little understanding about how to solve the problems. One of the phrases I heard at the time was that everything was "just too big to get done."

This backdrop led senior management to recognize that something systemic needed to change. And it needed to change fast. They knew it wasn't any individual problem causing such widespread issues but a collection of conditions. On the plus side, it was the push they needed to recognize that the company needed to adapt or it would continue to atrophy as competitors took the lead. To radically improve overall business performance, the company had to transform its operational, marketing, product development, merchandising, and human resources processes. No small feat.

In late fall 2007, I received a call from Priszm's president, Steve Langford, about a thorn the company had had in its side for several years involving cost overruns in its 450 KFC restaurants. These food losses were by no means destroying the company, but the company wanted to move the needle from good to great and hadn't been having success identifying the root causes, let alone any workable solutions. According to Langford, "We've been speculating for years about the cause but haven't found the root cause, let alone a solution."

During our conversation, we also discussed the KFC brand and Langford's hopes for Priszm's future. I could hear the passion in his voice about the brand. Clearly, he wanted—*needed*—change. So did many of his colleagues. They had done an impressive job identifying a number of issues and had worked like superheroes to improve them. But many of the changes failed to take root or didn't quite get to the heart of the matter. A desire for a radically different approach was what sparked his decision to call me. Langford needed financial results, sure, but he desperately wanted his people to think differently—that is, to think like he did. For Langford, the answers were clear, but for his people, they were clouded in the obscurity and complexity of the day-to-day operations.

Excited by the challenge, I was also delighted by the opportunity to return to Canada for a period, where I have so many wonderful friends and colleagues from my time working in Toronto. By the middle of September, we were forging ahead.

It Started with the Humble French Fry

Our first mandate involved cost overruns on french fries. Many theories had been floated, investigated, and pursued over the previous several years, but none had yielded results. We kicked off the french fry team with The Corporate Lab to offer team members insight into what their organization could look like, and followed up immediately with a thirty-day mandate to identify the root cause and fix the problem of french fry loss.

Prior to The Corporate Lab, Priszm senior management had developed conference room solutions to address the loss of french fries. Among the potential causes of the loss were vendors shortchanging restaurants on the weight of the frozen french fries that were being delivered or sloppy fry cooks spilling an unacceptable amount of the product. Never, however, had all of the people representing the different aspects of procuring, packaging, and serving the fries communicated with one another. So no one really knew the cause.

The team members were a great bunch of employees, including cashiers, cooks, restaurant managers, and more. They were invited because of their deep insights into day-to-day restaurant operations. I was the team coach.

Our project champion was company president Steve Langford. And our team leader, Brenda Wylie, was a purchasing manager who soon after the project became a senior manager of business development (in part because of her stellar performance during this and other Klapper projects).

Using The Klapper Institute's Results Triangle and the insights of frontline employees, we tested ideas and prototyped solutions. We monitored the process at the store level, audited food waste ourselves, even cut and taped experimental bags late into the evening until we verified the issue: the existing fry bags were causing employees to give customers approximately 4.2 ounces of fries instead of the appropriate 3.5 ounces. Who could blame them? The original bags were simply too big. According to one employee, "Who can look a customer in the eye and hand them an unfull bag of fries?"

When the team presented their findings to Langford, he laughed at the sheer simplicity. Well, he actually called it the "elegance" of the solution. Others on his team were less complimentary.

We heard, "It took twenty days to figure out the bag was too big?"

And, "I could have told you that on day one without the Lab!"

Yet they had tried to solve this issue for years before launching the team, with zero success. We often get responses like the above. In retrospect, the problem and its solution are often simple. Yet the "elegant" solutions are always hidden by the day-to-day noise that prevents the organization from seeing the simple answer right in front of it.

Through the insights offered by The Corporate Lab and the Results Triangle, which the team pursued during its thirty-day mandate (which they actually achieved in less than two weeks), the team identified and corrected the problem. Compared with the years and expense and wrong solutions of previous attempts to resolve this issue, our success was dazzling to everyone involved, from frontline employees to senior management. The ultimate savings in dollars was substantial—millions a year. Yet, the more important lesson that emerged from the undertaking, according to Steve Langford, was that "This approach deciphered a longtime vexing problem, and instead of making life more difficult for employees and management, it actually made it far simpler for everyone involved."

Langford adds, "Prior to KI, we used a theoretical, in-the-office approach to speculating about what the issue was. Or we brought in a team of consultants to theorize in more or less the same way as our own senior management. Brian brought in frontline KFC folks to figure out the precise cause and then created a tailor-made solution that really worked."

Moving On to Chicken

Our next mandate, which had also perplexed management for far too long, was the loss of up to 18 percent of chicken. The theories before our Corporate Lab on this issue (which involved a new team and thirty-day mandate) were that it was either being dropped or stolen. Or, possibly, the restaurants were being shortchanged by vendors. Or maybe the chicken was being weighed inaccurately. In other words, no one knew.

> **DID YOU KNOW?**
>
> Harland Sanders opened a gas station in 1930, and he served chicken dishes in his attached home. He opened his first restaurant in 1937, the year after he was made an honorary "Colonel" of Kentucky.[1]

Much like we had with the french fry mandate, we uncovered the truth in a short time and fixed the problem. At the risk of making the solution seem like no big deal (it was actually quite a big deal), here's the short version: employees were paid to work until ten o'clock at night, and so, understandably, wanted to get out right at ten. As a result, they were cooking up a final batch of chicken at around seven or eight p.m. and keeping it under heat lamps until closing time.

Less fresh chicken was less appealing to customers, resulting in lower sales and more discarded chicken at the end of the night. Now, in hindsight the solution might seem simple, and to an outsider looking in, it's tempting to judge those involved as being blind to an obvious problem. All I can say is that it wasn't obvious—not until we approached it with the right people and method. In the words of Brenda Wylie, team captain for this project, "We finally utilized the intellectual capital that the company had been investing in for years but never really tapped into." It's a phrase that has always stayed with me.

When the organization began paying closers for an extra hour of work so that they could cook fresh chicken—only in amounts that were needed—right up until the doors were locked for the night, the company created a win–win moment for everyone: an elegant, profitable, sustainable solution created from the inside.

Problem solved. Case closed. On to the next challenge.

We implemented several other significant changes for the organization as well, after which we were ready for something grand, a real game changer of a mandate. Sure, we had solved a number of real sticklers and were all darn proud, but the hero teams were hungry for bigger and bolder challenges. And of course word was spreading about the great work being done by these Klapper teams, and management was noticing. It seemed like everyone wanted to get involved. The wildfire of pull was spreading. Ideas were coming from everywhere. Energy was high.

Up to that point, Langford had been reluctant to engage in the complex enterprise-wide transformation that he knew the organization so desperately needed. The reason? He believed his people would never truly own the effort and it would just be another top-down, management-driven program that was destined to fail. Yet the results of the chicken and fry teams ignited the spark that Langford knew he needed to tackle the fundamental issues plaguing the company. He was ready. And he knew his people were, too.

Staying Focused on the Bigger Picture

Okay, you're thinking, so you helped them cut their french fry loss and throw away a little less chicken. Priszm's previous conditions weren't hurting them *that* much. Well, it actually was quite a big deal when you consider the inability of senior management to identify the issue and then change the underlying culture of the organization.

Management's old approach of trying to force change from on high hadn't worked. Their new approach of pulling change up from the bottom was revolutionary to them. And it was working. The Q-Loop approach of identifying an issue and looking within for ideas that get to the bottom of the problem; taking the solution to senior management for endorsement; and then driving it out to the organization using the employees who had once been resistors but were now passionate advocates was a hugely positive shift for Priszm. It helped establish Priszm's new approach to implementing change and getting buy-in from every level within the organization.

To a large extent, that was the real victory. Identifying one team of heroes after the next and exposing them to what was possible in The

Corporate Lab, then launching them immediately onto a project team to achieve mandate after mandate in less than thirty days, we were able to communicate success after success. This led in short order to a final mandate that was the boldest to date: creating a KFC Model Store that could prove many of the concepts we had prototyped and deliver them to a real audience in an actual KFC store.

A KFC Model Store Redefines Fast Food Dining

The idea started as one of those fleeting conversations in a hallway. The conversation took place between me and Brenda Wylie, the team captain I mentioned earlier, an individual who had been identified by senior management as an up-and-comer (for good reason, I learned quickly).

In that conversation, we agreed that we'd done some pretty great stuff, but now we needed to up the ante while there was momentum. I suggested that if we could experiment within a store to reconsider every aspect of the way a KFC restaurant is run, we could enhance the performance of that store and use it as a model for others. We knew we needed to get management to step away and let the frontline staff come up with the solutions. We believed that if we put rigor and dedication into it, we could fundamentally change the mechanics of the business to a point where it would be scalable and replicable across the organization nationally. And we could do it on a small budget.

The Model Store was to be no ordinary store, offering no ordinary experience to diners. It also would present an unmatched opportunity to the employees who had the chance to work there and play a vital role in implementing a whole host of breakthrough ideas.

In the spring of 2008, Priszm began the transformation of a KFC restaurant into a Model Store, a working restaurant and living experiment that would provide employees with insight about where value was created and lost. It also could serve as an incubator for new products, services, and cooking approaches.

The Model Store was an actual store, chosen because it was in the bottom 40 percent of performers and it was close to company headquarters, so it could be monitored easily. The Model Store itself was a mandate, with two goals: get it up and running in thirty days and on a budget of less than $20,000 (at the time, Priszm was running extremely lean).

Its purpose was to serve as an innovation lab—a typical restaurant in function and purpose, but atypical in that it could capture, document, and leverage learning for use in future broader-scale rollouts. After participants transformed this typical store, the lessons learned could be rolled out across the entire restaurant system.

Specifically, the Model Store was intended to provide the optimal dining experience for a KFC customer, which would include the hottest, freshest food served daily, unparalleled hospitality and service, an expanded variety of menu items, and a superbly clean and comfortable dining experience. The Model Store would also help to promote financial performance measures such as same-store sales growth, increased average check, and improved profitability. It was a big step up from cutting down on food waste, but was made possible by those earlier and meaningful successes

Priszm's team of heroes for this operations transformation team was composed of subject matter experts from across the company—representatives from consumer insights, product excellence, marketing, media, operations, supply chain, human resources, technology, finance planning, training, and store employees. The learning experience would have to be powerful to enable this diverse group of associates to rapidly solve its challenges. Because the team included the president as well as frontline store employees, it was critical to level the group, providing them with a shared experience that would allow them to become a high-performing work team immediately.

The client team developed the following success list to identify the values they expected:

1. All team members should receive a common experience, a common vision for the future, and an analytic tool set that all members understood and were excited about applying.
2. The entire team should internalize that all levels of management, including the chairman, understood and supported the vision.
3. The mandate had to be far reaching and take people out of their comfort zones, and the simulation should create a passion for developing the Model Store concept.
4. The approach must allow people to define new rules, to not be afraid of making a wrong decision, and to pursue a course of action.

To prepare to work in the Model Store, the Priszm team attended the two-day Corporate Lab, which helped them see what was possible, as it had already done for every previous team. According to Michelle Mihai, vice president of Priszm Brands, "Working in The Corporate Lab was one of the most difficult things I have ever had to do in my entire career. Once we successfully transformed NAVCorp, I had no doubt that we could apply the learning to fix Priszm…and we did!"

As we kicked off the transformation of the Model Store, I could sense the true passion on everyone's part. It was palpable. I had seen this sort of excitement before, but this day was deeply special, as this store in decline—representative of a number of other stores also in decline—was about to undergo real change. And the team was about to change with it.

The results perhaps speak for themselves. But before I tell you the results, let me share a sidebar. This mandate was one of the only ones I have ever been involved with that didn't hit its thirty-day target. We missed it by one day. The day before the scheduled relaunch of the store, it was robbed, and we had to delay one day for the police investigation.

Despite the hiccup, we did launch and in the first week, we had 33 percent growth in same-store sales, which was unheard of after a double-digit decline. By the time the project was completed, nine months later, we had implemented more than three hundred operational improvements and netted out as follows:

RESULTS AFTER NINE MONTHS OF KFC MODEL STORE OPERATION		
Performance Measure	**Model Store**	**Control Group**
Sales growth (versus prior year)	+14.9 percent	+4.6 percent
Store visits (versus prior year)	+6.3 percent	+0.5 percent
Average check (versus prior year)	+7.8 percent	+4.1 percent

Figure 8-1: KFC Model Store Operation Results

A tremendous success, right? Absolutely. Although most good stories surprise you in the end.

Here Comes the Twist

Many of the changes that were so boldly and successfully implemented within the Model Store were not ultimately rolled out through the other KFC outlets. For reasons that had nothing to do with the Model Store project or any of the other mandates we successfully implemented, Priszm sold a number of restaurants a few years later and underwent a restructuring.

Great case study, right? As you may have noticed, I'm not always one for playing precisely by the rules, so why should I end my book according to the rules?

See, beneath the numbers and facts were the people who were fundamentally changed by the experience and the processes that were vastly and measurably improved. We had *tremendous* successes along the way and all felt unshakably poised to take the KFC brand to ever greater heights. It would be arrogant for me to suggest that if these changes had been more fully embraced by the larger organization and fully embedded, the outcome of the organization might have been different. So I won't make such a suggestion (too late?).

Creating a Model Store truly was a first step in the transformation of Priszm. The store excelled for years following the launch on all operating measures, including sales growth, return visits, and operating profit, and at least some of the concepts learned were rolled out across other KFC stores.

If this grassroots mind-set shift had been given full support and taken root throughout the organization, who knows? It could have been the blueprint for bringing profitable ideas to market in a swift and scalable way. And so I share this story for two reasons: one, to demonstrate the tremendously valuable work that is accomplished as a result of the Q-Loop. Two, as a cautionary tale against, well, being overly cautionary. (Interesting sidenote: In 2011, Priszm's president, Steve Langford, joined The Klapper Institute.)

Greatness comes to the bold. Be bold. So many of my clients have been and continue to be, and it has served them well. When someone writes a book many decades from now about organizations that have weathered the years by remaining nimble, will you be on the list? Will you have left your competitors in the dust? Will you have achieved the ability to produce lasting change?

It's now up to you.

FINAL THOUGHTS

This journey around the Q-Loop together has been deeply rewarding for me. And I thank you for traveling it. I can only hope that it brings you some of the satisfaction and success that I have witnessed in my clients. I know that it has brought me great joy and fulfillment in the many rides it has taken me on over the years. None has been the same and none has failed to thrill me.

Now, I would never claim that transformational change is easy or that this book will pave a perfectly smooth path for you. Change is quite simply one of the most challenging journeys an organization will ever take. But for more than twenty years, I've had the pleasure to study and work with organizations that have effectively implemented major strategy and process initiatives, and one of the common elements that has enabled successful and lasting change with all of these organization has been the use of the Q-Loop.

Increasingly, the Q-Loop isn't a nice-to-have feature for organizations that manage to find the time to get around to using it. It's an imperative. I said it near the beginning of the book, but it bears repeating now that we are approaching the end: organizations that fail to adapt to the changing landscape risk falling irrevocably behind their competitors.

The first steps you must take to avoid this plight are recognizing the essential need to adapt, looking for an influx of targeted and strategic ideas, and learning to benefit from your organization's collective IQ. It's therefore no accident that this is the content of the first part of this book. The second critical steps (and the second part of this book) are embracing an effective process for selecting change mandates and achieving them swiftly. Finally, you must embed this ability irrevocably into your organization, as described in the last chapter. Together, these steps form the Q-Loop.

BEFORE THE Q-LOOP	AFTER THE Q-LOOP
Satisfy your customers	DELIGHT YOUR CUSTOMERS
Offer products and services	DELIVER SOLUTIONS AND GREAT EXPERIENCES
Tolerate incrementalism	DELIVER REVOLUTIONARY IDEAS AT A FURIOUS PACE
Accept that good is good	RECOGNIZE THAT GOOD IS THE ENEMY OF GREAT
Run away from failure	ASSERTIVELY PURSUE FAILURE TO ACHIEVE SUCCESS

At the end of each chapter, I've offered you a snapshot of the chapter as well as a brief preview of the next chapter. Well, there are no next chapters. There's just you and your colleagues and your organization and your great ability to now implement and sustain change. Which means that what's coming up next is the most exciting part of all.

It's you... taking what you've learned from this book and diving in feet first to discover a better future for your organization.

While it's extremely tempting for me to slip into grandiose language at this point—and I would mean every word of it as I said fare thee well or bid you Godspeed—let me perhaps err on the side of understatement when I simply say that I couldn't be happier for you or more confident that you are now capable of boosting your organization to the next level and beyond. And I believe you can do it long into the future.

Please let me know how you are doing at *bklapper@theklapperinstitute.com*. Your wisdom and insights, like those of my clients, are always enlightening to me and are always such a delight to hear.

For now, I'll just wish you all of my best and thank you deeply for this journey we were able to take together. Let me leave you by reversing a concept from earlier in the book, where I shared with you the formula for failure. Let me now show you the formula for success.

+ *See the need for change*
+ *Be open to new ideas*
+ *Be willing to take risk*
+ *Move quickly and decisively*
+ *Set audacious goals*
+ *Show employees the "art of the possible"*
+ *Empower employees to ideate and implement*
+ *Turn resistance into passion*
+ *Embrace the Results Triangle*
+ *Repeat success ad infinitum*

= *Ability to produce lasting change*

ENDNOTES

Chapter 1

1. Rothschild, William. *The Secret to GE's Success.* New York: McGraw-Hill Companies, 2007.
2. "Why It's Not a Blockbuster IPO," last modified August 1, 1999, http://www.businessweek.com/stories/1999-08-01/why-its-not-a-blockbuster-ipo.
3. "Dish Network Wins Blockbuster Auction With $320 Million Bid," last modified April 6, 2011, http://www.bloomberg.com/news/2011-04-06/dish-network-said-to-win-blockbuster-auction-at-320-million.html.
4. "Negative Exposure for Kodak," last modified October 20, 2011, http://www.nytimes.com/2011/10/21/business/kodaks-bet-on-its-printers-fails-to-quell-the-doubters.html?pagewanted=all.
5. "Kodak: 130 Years of History," last modified January 19, 2012, http://www.telegraph.co.uk/finance/newsbysector/retailandconsumer/9024539/Kodak-130-years-of-history.html.
6. "Putting Science to Work," last modified 2011, http://thechallenge.dupont.com/dupont/putting-science-to-work.php.
7. "Innovation Starts Here," last modified 2012, http://www2.dupont.com/Phoenix_Heritage/en_US/index.html.
8. "Strategic IQ: Creating Smarter Corporations," last modified 2011, http://www.exed.hbs.edu/assets/Documents/wellsQAsa11.pdf.
9. "Samsung Takes Cell Phone Market Lead from Nokia," last modified April 27, 2012, http://money.cnn.com/2012/04/27/technology/nokia-samsung/index.htm.
10. "Current Thinking," last modified June 3, 2007, http://www.nytimes.com/2007/06/03/magazine/03wwln-essay-t.html?_r=0.
11. "The Best CEO's Grasp Change with Enthusiasm," http://seec.schulich.yorku.ca/best_ceo_enthusiasm.aspx.

Chapter 2

1. "Robert Half Survey: Lack of New Ideas, Red Tape Greatest Barriers to Innovation," last modified April 4, 2012, http://www.prnewswire.com/news-releases/robert-half-survey-lack-of-new-ideas-red-tape-greatest-barriers-to-innovation-146074815.html.

2. "You Call That Innovation?" last modified May 23, 2012, http://online.wsj
.com/article/SB10001424052702304791704577418250902309914.html.

3. "Post It Note," http://inventors.about.com/od/pstartinventions/a/post_it_
note.htm.

4. "The Google Way: Give Engineers Room," last modified October 21, 2007,
http://www.nytimes.com/2007/10/21/jobs/21pre.html.

5. "A Short History of Xerox PARC," last modified September 20, 2010, http://
features.techworld.com/sme/3240287/a-short-history-of-xerox-parc/.

6. Finkelstein, Sydney. *Why Smart Executives Fail: And What You Can Learn
from Their Mistakes.* New York: Penguin Group, 2003.

7. "Rubbermaid: About Us," http://www.rubbermaid.com/mediaCenter/
aboutUS/Pages/AboutUs.aspx.

8. Sherri Daye, "Sonic's First Fifty," *QSR,* September 2003, 34.

9. "The Value of Edison's Inventions to the World," http://www.web-books
.com/Classics/ON/B0/B128/EdisonC27.html.

10. Thomke, Stefan H. *Experimentation Matters: Unlocking the Potential of New
Technologies for Innovation.* Boston: Harvard Business School Publishing
Corporation, 2003.

11. "Gaining the Edge in New Business Development," last modified 2007, http://
www.lek.com/sites/default/files/JBS_Gaining_the_edge.pdf.

12. "IBM Logo," http://www.logoblog.org/ibm-logo.php.

13. "15 Scientific Facts About Creativity," http://www.onlineuniversities.com/
15-scientific-facts-about-creativity.

14. Winchester, Simon. *The Professor and the Madman: A Tale of Murder, Insan-
ity, and the Making of the Oxford English Dictionary.* New York: Harper
Perennial, 1999.

15. "BP Oil Spill: Disaster by Numbers," last modified September 14, 2010, http://
www.independent.co.uk/environment/bp-oil-spill-disaster-by-numbers-
2078396.html.

16. "Information Anxiety," last modified September 1998, http://www.theatlantic
.com/past/docs/issues/98sep/copy3.htm.

17. Edwin A. Locke, Vinod K. Jain, (1995) "Organizational Learning and Continuous Improvement," *International Journal of Organizational Analysis,*
Vol. 3 Iss: 1, pp. 45 – 68.

18. Pink, Daniel. *Drive: The Surprising Truth About What Motivates Us.* New
York: Riverhead Books, 2009.

Chapter 3

1. "Social Knows: Employee Engagement Statistics," last updated August 8, 2011,
http://www.thesocialworkplace.com/2011/08/08/social-knows-employee-
engagement-statistics-august-2011-edition/.

2. "Social Knows: Employee Engagement Statistics."

3. "Band Aid," http://www.princeton.edu/~achaney/tmve/wiki100k/docs/Band-Aid.html.

4. "Institute for Management Studies: The Idea-Driven Organization: Tapping Employee Ideas to Improve Performance," last updated January 24, 2012, http://digest.stjohns.edu/admin_staff/ev_hr_120124_ims.stj?context_date=1/24/2012.

5. "Social Knows: Employee Engagement Statistics."

6. "First Place for Continental Idea Management," last updated May 3, 2011, http://www.conti-online.com/generator/www/com/en/continental/press portal/themes/press_releases/1_topics/work_life/pr_2011_05_03_CIM_en, version=13.html.

7. Yasuda, Yuzo. *40 Years, 20 Million Ideas: The Toyota Suggestion System.* Cambridge: Productivity Press, 1990.

8. Robinson, Alan G. and Dean M. Schroeder. *Ideas Are Free: How the Idea Revolution Is Liberating People and Transforming Organizations.* San Francisco: Berrett-Koehler Publishers, 2004.

9. "Clarion Hotels: Continuous Improvement of the Way We Take Care of Our Guests," http://www.c2management.se/en/clients/36-clarion-hotels-vi-blir-staendigt-baettre-pa-att-ta-hand-om-vara-gaester.

10. "For Bright Ideas, Ask the Staff," last modified October 17, 2011, http://online.wsj.com/article/SB10001424052970204774604576631063939483984.html.

11. "True Innovation," last modified February 25, 2012, http://www.nytimes.com/2012/02/26/opinion/sunday/innovation-and-the-bell-labs-miracle.html?pagewanted=all.

12. "'Innovation Initiative' Underway for Health Records Improvements," last modified February 18, 2010, http://www1.va.gov/opa/pressrel/pressrelease.cfm?id=1851.

13. Robinson, *Ideas Are Free.*

14. "Management by Consciousness: A Value-Oriented Spiritual Approach ," last modified November-December 2004, http://www.techmonitor.net/tm/images/0/09/04nov_dec_managing_innovation.pdf.

15. "Small Ideas Are Big Hits," last modified August 1, 1993, http://www.inc.com/magazine/19930801/3666.html.

16. "Management Philosophy," http://www.idemitsu.com/company/policy/index.html.

17. Dinero, Donald. *Training Within Industry: The Foundation of Lean.* Cambridge: Productivity Press, 2005.

18. Robinson, Alan G. *Corporate Creativity: How Innovation & Improvement Actually Happen.* San Francisco: Berrett-Koehler Publishers, 1998.

19. "Too Many Companies Turn a Deaf Ear to Employee Ideas," last modified October 1, 2001, http://www.bizjournals.com/jacksonville/stories/2001/10/01/smallb4.html?page=all.

20. Thomas, Martin. *Crowd Surfing: Surviving and Thriving in the Age of Consumer Empowerment.* London: A&C Black, 2008.

21. "Companies Are Implementing More of Staffers' Suggestions," last modified June 29, 1992, http://articles.baltimoresun.com/1992-06-29/business/1992181116_1_ employee-suggestions-employee-suggestion-programs-prunty.

22. "Managing the Mandate to Innovate: A Step-by-Step Guide," last modified June 27, 2005, http://www.computerworld.com/s/article/102764/Managing_ the_Mandate_to_Innovate_A_Step_by_Step_Guide.

23. "How to Manage Innovative Ideas in the Modern Enterprise," last modified June 9, 2011, http://gigaom.com/2011/06/09/how-to-manage-innovative-ideas-in-the-modern-enterprise/.

24. "What's in Amazon's Box? Instant Gratification," last modified November 24, 2010, http://www.businessweek.com/magazine/content/10_49/ b4206039292096.htm.

25. "What's in Amazon's Box? Instant Gratification."

Chapter 4

1. Lombardi, Vince. *The Lombardi Rules: 26 Lessons from Vince Lombardi—the World's Greatest Coach*. New York: McGraw-Hill Companies, 2003.

2. Johnson, Neville. *The John Wooden Pyramid of Success: The Authorized Biography, Philosophy and Ultimate Guide to Life, Leadership, Friendship and Love of the Greatest Coach in the History of Sports*. Beverly Hills: Cool Titles, 2003.

3. "Our History—How It Began." http://www.pg.com/en_US/downloads/ media/Fact_Sheets_CompanyHistory.pdf.

4. "Lou Holtz and Leadership—What Does Your Team Expect from You?" last modified April 22, 2009, http://canadaultimate.blogspot.com/2009/04/lou-holtz-and-leadership-what-does-your.html.

5. "Corporate Transformation Under Pressure," last modified April 2009, http://www.mckinseyquarterly.com/Corporate_transformation_under_ pressure_2308.

Chapter 5

1. "MIT 150: 150 Fascinating, Fun, Important, Interesting, Lifesaving, Life-altering, Bizarre and Bold Ways that MIT Has Made a Difference," last modified May 15, 2011, http://www.boston.com/news/education/higher/specials/ mit150/mitlist/?page=full.

2. "California Nuke Simulator Is World's Most Powerful Computer," last modified June 18, 2012, http://www.wired.com/wiredenterprise/2012/06/ top500-llnl/.

3. "The Marshmallow Challenge," http://marshmallowchallenge.com/Welcome .html.

Chapter 6

1. "Chinese Builders Construct 30-Story Hotel—in 15 Days," last modified January 10, 2012, http://newsfeed.time.com/2012/01/10/chinese-builders-construct-30-story-hotel-in-15-days/.
2. "FedEx Logo," http://www.logoblog.org/fedex-logo.php.
3. "15 Logos with Hidden Messages," last modified , August 24, 2010, http://webdesignledger.com/inspiration/15-logos-with-hidden-messages.
4. "Inside Amazon's Idea Machine: How Bezos Decodes The Customer," last modified April 4, 2012, http://www.forbes.com/sites/georgeanders/2012/04/04/inside-amazon/.
5. "From Cost Center to Profit Center: Optimizing Your Contact Center for Maximum Results," last modified 2011, http://archway.com/Portals/0/Documents/Whitepapers/From%20Cost%20Center%20to%20Profit%20Center.pdf.
6. "History of Antiseptics," http://inventors.about.com/library/inventors/blantisceptics.htm.
7. "How Braille Began," http://www.brailler.com/braillehx.htm.
8. "Cheap, Fast, and in Control: How Tech Aids Innovation," last modified August 11, 2003, http://hbswk.hbs.edu/item/3627.html#6
9. "Creation Myth," last modified May 16, 2011, http://www.gladwell.com/2011/2011_05_16_a_creationmyth.html.
10. "Why CEOs Fail," last modified June 21, 1999, http://money.cnn.com/magazines/fortune/fortune_archive/1999/06/21/261696/index.htm.
11. Kotter, John P. *Leading Change*. Boston: Harvard Business Review Press, 1996.
12. "The Places of Books in the Age of Electronic Reproduction," last modified spring 1994, http://people.ischool.berkeley.edu/~nunberg/places3.html

Chapter 7

1. "15 Facts About McDonald's That Will Blow Your Mind," last modified November 25, 2011, http://www.businessinsider.com/facts-about-mcdonalds-blow-your-mind-2011-11?op=1.
2. "Shigeki Terashi Helped Return Toyota Motor Engineering & Manufacturing to Full Production," last modified April 1, 2011, http://www.sbnonline.com/2012/04/shigeki-terashi-helped-return-toyota-motor-engineering-manufacturing-to-full-production/.

Chapter 8

1. "How KFC Became the Biggest Fried Chicken Joint on the Planet," last modified July 18, 2012, http://www.businessinsider.com/kfc-history-2012-7?op=1.

INDEX